D0627277

7/95

Jamaica Kincaid

Twayne's United States Authors Series

Frank Day, Editor

Clemson University

TUSAS 646

Jamaica Kincaid

Jamaica Kincaid

Diane Simmons

Upsala College

Twayne Publishers • New York
Maxwell Macmillan Canada • Toronto
Maxwell Macmillan International • New York Oxford Singapore Sydney

Twayne's United States Authors Series No. 646

Jamaica Kincaid
Diane Simmons

Twayne Publishers
Macmillan Publishing Company
866 Third Avenue
New York, New York 10022

Maxwell Macmillan Canada, Inc.
1200 Eglinton Avenue East
Suite 200
Don Mills, Ontario M3C 3N1

Library of Congress Cataloging-in-Publication Data

Simmons, Diane, 1948–
    Jamaica Kincaid / Diane Simmons.
        p.   cm.—(Twayne's United States authors series ; TUSAS 646)
    Includes bibliographical references and index.
    ISBN 0-8057-3994-7 (alk. paper)
    1. Kincaid, Jamaica—Criticism and interpretation. 2. Antiguans in literature.
3. Antigua—In literature. I. Title. II. Series.
PR9275.A583K567   1994
813—dc20   94-25608
                                              CIP

Z
KINCAID
S

1284258

The paper used in this publication meets the minimum requirements of American National Standard for Information Sciences—Permanence of Paper for Printed Library Materials. ANSI Z3948–1984.∞™

10 9 8 7 6 5 4 3 2 1 (hc)

Printed in the United States of America

Contents

Acknowledgments

My thanks to Jamaica Kincaid for taking perfectly good gardening time to talk to me one June morning; to Mickey Pearlman for helping to get this project—and so many others—off the ground; to June Bobb for generously giving advice and for sharing information on West Indian writers; to Neal Tolchin for always being so solid; to Barbara Webb and James De Jongh for reading and advising; to my editors Frank Day and Mark Zadrozny for being refreshingly professional; and, most of all, to my husband, Burt Kimmelman, for supporting me with an array of editorial, computer, culinary, and child-care skills.

Chronology:

1949   Born Elaine Potter Richardson on the Caribbean island of Antigua.

1965   Leaves Antigua to work as an au pair in New York.

1969–1970   Studies photography at the New School for Social Research in New York City and at Franconia College in New Hampshire.

1973   Publishes "When I Was 17," a series of interviews, in *Ingenue* magazine. Changes her name to Jamaica Kincaid.

1974   Meets William Shawn, editor of the *New Yorker*. Publishes "West Indian Weekend" in the *New Yorker*, the first of 85 unsigned "Talk of the Town" pieces published through 1983.

1976   Becomes a staff writer at the *New Yorker*.

1978   Writes her first fiction, "Girl," later published in the *New Yorker* and in the collection *At the Bottom of the River*.

1979   Marries composer Allen Shawn, son of William Shawn.

1983   Wins the Morton Dauwen Zabel Award of the American Academy and Institute of Arts and Letters for *At the Bottom of the River* and is nominated for PEN/Faulkner Award.

1985   Publishes *Annie John*, which is a finalist for international Ritz Paris Hemingway Award. Gives birth to a daughter, Annie.

1988   Publishes *A Small Place*. Gives birth to a son, Harold.

1990   Publishes *Lucy*.

1992   Publishes the first of a series of articles in the *New Yorker* on gardening.

1994   *Autobiography of My Mother* currently scheduled for publication in Fall, 1994.

Chapter One

A Paradise Lost

At heart Jamaica Kincaid's work is not about the charm of a Caribbean childhood, though her first and best-known novel, *Annie John*, may leave this impression. Nor is it about colonialism, though her angry essay *A Small Place* accuses the reader of continuing the exploitation begun by Columbus. Nor, finally, is Kincaid's work about black and white in America, though her novel *Lucy* runs a rich white urban family through the shredder of a young black au pair's rage. Kincaid's work is about loss, an all but unbearable fall from a paradise partially remembered, partially dreamed, a state of wholeness, in which things are unchangeably themselves and division is unknown.

This sense of betrayal, which permeates Kincaid's work, is explored first in the treachery of a once-adored mother. In Kincaid's first book, the collection of surrealistic short stories *At the Bottom of the River*, a girl yearns for an impossible return to the perfect world that existed before the "betrayal" of birth and for union with a mother figure who will "every night, over and over, . . . tell me something that begins, 'Before you were born.'"[1] But the yearning for a lost maternal paradise is inextricably linked to betrayal, and elsewhere in *At the Bottom of the River* the mother is shown methodically transforming herself into a serpent, growing "plates of metal-colored scales on her back" and flattening her head "so that her eyes, which were by now ablaze, sat on top of her head and spun like two revolving balls" (*BR*, 55).

In *Annie John*, a more conventionally narrative coming-of-age book, the treachery of a once-adoring mother is spelled out. As the child begins to reach puberty, the mother suddenly turns on her. The mother, who had previously seen her daughter as beautiful and perfect, now sees the child as a mass of imperfection and immorality. At the same time that she imposes rules and regimens designed to turn the girl into a "young lady," the mother also communicates that this project is doomed, that no amount of training can overcome what she now perceives to be the girl's true nature, that of a "slut."

While betrayal by a beloved mother is a theme that echoes throughout Kincaid's work, this first treachery is matched by another, that of the

British colonial power, which dominated the Antigua of Kincaid's child-hood. The young protagonist of *Annie John* enjoys the prestige of being a top student. But approval and praise are withdrawn when Annie, in her growing awareness that she is the descendant of people whose enslavement was the result of European "discovery," treats a picture of Christopher Columbus with mild disrespect. As a child of the colonial system, Annie is faced with a dilemma similar to that which she has begun to face when dealing with her mother: both powers, maternal and imperial, demand childlike devotion and unquestioning trust, and both turn on the girl in retaliatory fury at the slightest hint of mature awareness. To be acknowledged, loved, and rewarded, then, she must betray her own maturing self. The result is a confusion about where the self really lies: "Sometimes, what with our teachers and our books, it was hard for us to tell on which side we really now belonged—with the master or with the slaves."[2]

Like the betraying mother, the colonial system, in pretending to nurture the child, actually steals her from herself. In the colonial system imposed by the British on the Caribbean, wrote Craig Tapping, speaking of both *Annie John* and *In the Castle of My Skin*, George Lamming's novel of a Caribbean childhood, "the self is faced with extinction by the very processes of acculturation which all who nurture the child commend."[3] Only imitation and blind acquiescence are acceptable, not the questioning gaze of an emerging intelligence.

The themes of betrayal and of an increasing anger at having been somehow trapped into turning against oneself explode in *A Small Place*, in which the author revisits her home, the island of Antigua, after an absence of 20 years. The island is now self-governing, but white tourists have replaced the departed British as the dominant group. As the tourists turn the islanders into holiday attractions, the islanders retaliate in kind, reducing the tourist into a dehumanized object. "An ugly thing," Kincaid wrote, "that is what you are when you become a tourist, an ugly empty thing, a stupid thing . . . and it will never occur to you that the people who inhabit the place in which you have just paused cannot stand you."[4]

If the white tourists in Antigua are excoriated, the black inhabitants are not spared Kincaid's wrath as they, in some areas, act out the roles of incompetence and dishonesty written for them by the English and, in others, emulate imperial rapacity. The postindependence schools are so bad that Kincaid, with her preindependence education, is shocked. And the government of Antigua is so patently dishonest that "the answer on every Antiguan's lips to the question, 'What is going on here now?' is 'The government is corrupt. Them are thief, them are big thief.' Imagine, then, the bitterness and the shame in me as I tell you this" (*SP*, 41). Once again the betrayer is, in part, the self.

In *Lucy* the themes of loss and betrayal are continued, though the title character is no longer in the Caribbean but has come to work as an au pair in a big American city resembling New York. The sense of loss may be even more powerful here than in Kincaid's other works, as the rich beloved contradiction of the childhood world is not only figuratively but also literally lost. Lucy—named, her mother has told her, for Lucifer—has been expelled from both the Caribbean and her mother's life. Warm, vivid Antigua has been replaced by the pale chill of a North American winter. Lucy's mother, source of all intelligence, power, beauty, and magic, has been replaced by Lucy's wealthy employer, the affectionate but sheltered and naive Mariah, who proffers books on feminism to help Lucy over her deep sense of loss and despair. In one way, Kincaid's young protagonist has, by leaving home, triumphed over her mother's wish to keep her forever infantilized or criminalized. Still, she is threatened by the mother's power. She keeps her mother's letters but does not open them: "I knew that if I read only one, I would die from longing for her."[5]

If Lucy has not entirely freed herself of her mother, neither is she free of the destructive legacy of a colonial education. When Mariah, brimming with delight in the pale spring of the Northeast, introduces Lucy to her favorite place, a grove of daffodils, Lucy is filled with rage. She has never seen a daffodil before but had been forced to memorize a long poem about daffodils as part of her British education, an education that, as a matter of course, expected students to ignore their own lush flora and to study and celebrate a plant they would probably never see. Though Mariah's intentions are innocent, even loving, Lucy wants only to take a scythe and "kill" the flowers. Part of her fury is at how "simple" they look, as if "made to erase a complicated and unnecessary idea" (*Lucy*, 29), the complicated idea of dominance. The colonial education, which has forced the girl first to love daffodils, then to hate them, creates a chasm between her and the well-meaning Mariah. "I felt sorry that I had cast her beloved daffodils in a scene she had never considered, a scene of conquered and conquests; a scene of brutes masquerading as angels and angels portrayed as brutes. . . . It wasn't her fault. It wasn't my fault. But nothing could change the fact that where she saw beautiful flowers I saw sorrow and bitterness. The same thing could cause us to shed tears, but those tears would not taste the same" (*Lucy*, 30). Here, too, neither the source of suffering nor its redress is simple.

While the themes of loss, betrayal, and self-betrayal permeate these works, this is probably not what draws most readers to Kincaid's writing. Rather, readers are struck first by the language, which reviewers frequently describe in terms of poetry, demonstrating a "joy in the sheer sounds of words."[6] Kincaid's language can be examined in a number of ways. It has been claimed as particularly "feminine," the "language of sounds and silence" of the nursery, "which stands before and beyond the rational signifying words of the father." Kincaid's style has also been described as "a successful example of [the] Afro-American rhetorical strategy [as] parody, repetition, inversion mark every single movement of Kincaid's narrative."[7] "Girl," the first piece in the collection *At the Bottom of the River* and Kincaid's first story to be published in the *New Yorker*, which later published virtually all of her fiction, is described as "a rhythm so strong it seemed to be hypnosis, aimed at magically chanting out bits of the subconscious."[8] Published as a one-page-long sentence, the piece begins,

> Wash the white clothes on Monday and put them on the stone heap; wash the color clothes on Tuesday and put them on the clothesline to dry; don't walk barehead in the hot sun; cook pumpkin fritters in very hot sweet oil; soak your little cloths right after you take them off; when buying cotton to make yourself a nice blouse, be sure that it doesn't have gum on it, because that way it won't hold up well after a wash; soak salt fish overnight before you cook it; is it true that you sing benna in Sunday school?; always eat your food in such a way that it won't turn someone else's stomach; on Sundays try to walk like a lady and not like the slut you are so bent on becoming. (*BR*, 3)

While the style may mesmerize, may have such power as to seem an end in itself, the careful reader begins to see that Kincaid's language may be the most powerful symbol of all for the themes of loss and betrayal in a world divided against itself. In this passage, as the proprieties of Europe are positioned against the sensualities of Africa, the voice of the nurturing mother suddenly wheels to attack as the sentence turns upon itself. A Kincaid sentence, as West Indian poet Derek Walcott wrote, constantly "heads toward its own contradiction."[9] Finally, it may be that it is in Kincaid's sentences, if not in her stories, that a kind of resolution to the crisis of loss and betrayal is achieved. Here at least the contradictions are held in suspension.

The fact that Kincaid's work is so frequently its own contradiction may explain the difficulty critics have had in categorizing it. Intensely personal, psychologically dense, Kincaid's writing "does not fit in to any of the fashionable schools of Caribbean writing" that are preoccupied with racial and social identity.[10] Nor can she be easily categorized as a black or feminist writer: Kincaid does not feel the need to "delineate" her world "sociologically," wrote black studies scholar and critic Henry Louis Gates, Jr. "She never feels the necessity of claiming the existence of a black world or a female sensibility. She assumes them both." The ability to make this assumption marks a "distinct departure," in Gates's view, and he compared her to another writer, Toni Morrison, who also assumes her world. With writers like these, "we can get beyond the large theme of racism and get to deeper themes of how black people love and cry and live and die. Which, after all, is what art is all about" (quoted in Garis, 70).

While none of Kincaid's fiction is formally described as autobiographical, it seems clear that her three fictional works, when compared with stories Kincaid has told of herself in her journalism and interviews, are based on the personal odyssey of a girl who began life as Elaine Potter Richardson in 1949 on the tiny island of Antigua, a girl who adored her tall, beautiful, intelligent Dominican mother but who somehow lost that mother's love, a girl who left the Caribbean to work as an au pair for an American family, and who, nurtured by the anonymity and freedom of New York City in the 1970s, reinvented herself as the writer Jamaica Kincaid.

Autobiography is the only sort of writing that really interests Kincaid. Asked to discuss the extent to which her work is autobiographical, she said, "I started to write out of this need, I suppose, to settle demons and settle scores and all sorts of things. So . . . I'm driven to write, so it has to be autobiographical. . . . I don't have any other reason to write. I'm not interested in things for their own sake. I'm only interested in explaining something for myself." While Kincaid said that everything she writes is autobiographical, it is "also fiction. It wouldn't hold up in a court of law."[11]

While the novel *Lucy* is based on Kincaid's first years in the United States, the experiences and emotions of a young West Indian woman living in the New York City of the 1970s are also explored in nonfictional form in an article entitled "Jamaica Kincaid's New York," published in *Rolling Stone* magazine. In both works there is a conscious sense of self-invention. In the *Rolling Stone* piece Kincaid wrote, "My mother sees my life in New York as turning against her. . . . She must know that I couldn't have lost one self and found another and still pass for a nonlunatic in any other place but New York."[12] At the end of *Lucy* the young woman sees that despite the intense longing she feels for her mother and the life she has left behind, she is becoming someone new: "But the things I could not see about myself, the things I could not put my hands on—those things had changed, and I did not yet know them well. I understood that I was inventing myself, and that I was doing this more in the way of a painter than in the way of a scientist" (*Lucy*, 134).

Elaine Potter Richardson was born in 1949 to what she has called "poor, ordinary" people:

> My mother's family comes from Dominica; they were land peasants. They had a lot of land, which they lost through my aunt making a bad marriage and my mother falling out with her family. My mother says that my real father can't even read, but he made a lot of money. . . . The man I speak of as my father [in my works] is really my stepfather. I grew up thinking he was my father. . . . I know a sort of person who is my father. We see each other, but I can't get myself to call him "father." He's sort of typical of West Indian men: I mean, they have children, but they never seem to connect themselves to these children.[13]

Kincaid's stepfather was a carpenter, and her mother kept house. As an only child, the young Kincaid felt happy and loved. But when she was nine, the first of her three brothers was born and her mother's attention seemed to shift. At the same time, the young girl became gradually aware of the islanders' subservience to the British, a status others seemed to accept. She began to be seen as a problem in school and, as punishment, was forced to memorize long chunks of John Milton's *Paradise Lost*. If her precocity got her into trouble with her teachers, it did not necessarily endear her to her fellow students: "I was very bright; I was always being made fun of for it" (Simmons).

The accounts of her childhood that Kincaid has given in interviews and articles are not only of conflict and loss, for they are intermixed with memories of a place whose natural beauty sometimes takes on a kind of spiritual quality and of a people who so fully accept and internalize this quality that they need not recognize it intellectually or label it. Kincaid celebrated this relation to physical beauty in one of her early contributions to "Notes and Comment" from "Talk of the Town" in the *New Yorker*:

> Every morning—workday, Saturday or Sunday—the whole island was alive by six o'clock. People got up early on weekdays to go to work or to school; they got up early on Saturday to go to market; and they got up early on Sunday to go to church.
>
> It is true that the early morning is the most beautiful time of the day on the island. The sun has just come up and is immediately big and bright, the way the sun always is on an island, but the air is still cool from the night; the sky is a deep cool blue (like the sea, it gets lighter as the day wears on, and then it gets darker, until by midnight it looks black); the red in the hibiscus and the flamboyant flowers seems redder; the green of the trees and grass seems greener. . . . But it wasn't to admire any of these things that people got up so early. I had never, in all the time I lived there, heard anyone say, "What a beautiful morning." Once, just the way I had read it in a book, I stretched and said to my mother, "Oh, isn't it a really lovely morning?" She didn't reply to that at all, but she pulled my eyelids this way and that and then said that my sluggish liver was getting even more sluggish.[14]

While Kincaid seems to suggest here that dwelling amid great natural beauty imparts a spiritual quality to life, she also sees, in a later work, that the same beauty can be a kind of "prison": "What might it do [to people] to live in such heightened, intense surroundings day after day?" (*SP*, 79). One thing it might do, she speculates, is keep them trapped in the moment, never able to step back to analyze or shape their own experience and therefore seldom able to control it.

The Caribbean of Kincaid's childhood, as seen through her interviews and journalism, is not exclusively female. There are gentle portrayals of a carpenter-father (the island's "second- best"), his shop where "everything was some shade of brown," and his convalescence from a heart condition, which happened simultaneously with his daughter's recovery from a case of hookworm. The two invalids would lie on their backs on the parents' bed, their feet on the windowsill in the sun, until Kincaid's mother came in and asked them to take their feet off the windowsill, and "we would do it right away, but as soon as she left we would put them back."[15] Kincaid's father (i.e., stepfather) talked to her about his own father's work on the Panama Canal—as a child Kincaid had the impression that her grandfather had built the canal more or less by himself—

and about the Americans, or, as he called them, the "Yanks." Kincaid's stepfather, who had worked as a carpenter on an American base in Antigua during World War II and who enjoyed American movies such as the Bing Crosby and Bob Hope "Road" movies, would tell his daughter "how funny and great and attractive and smart Americans in general were. . . . At the end of every story about Americans . . . he would say, 'Oh, the Yanks are a crazy bunch, but they have ideas, and you can't stop a man when he has ideas.' But the thing my father said about Americans that made me love them the most was, 'The Yanks are great. Listen, if a Yank ever asks you if you can do something and you can't do it, don't say "No," say "I'll try." ' "[16]

Kincaid's childhood world is not, then, exclusively female, but it is predominantly so, as demonstrated by the opening sentence of one of her earliest pieces of fiction, a story called "Antigua Crossings": "The Caribbean Sea is so big, and so blue, and so deep and so warm, and so unpredictable, and so inviting, and so dangerous, and so beautiful. This is exactly the way I feel about all the women in my own family."[17]

One aspect of this unpredictability and danger was the women's practice of obeah, an African-rooted belief, similar to voodoo. For believers, Kincaid said, "everything has a life of its own, it's chaotic, it's subject to all sorts of laws. [That is] one of the beauties and one of the attractions, it is subject to laws that not everybody knows, so you can do something to someone because only you know how it works, and when you do it to them, only you know what it is you are doing. The person you are doing it to then has to find out how it works to counteract. It's a secret. It's never done out in the open" (Simmons).

Both Kincaid's mother and grandmother were believers in obeah. Kincaid's grandmother, like the grandmother in *Annie John*, was married to a Methodist minister and followed his faith for a time but reverted to a belief in obeah after her son died, apparently as a result of a magic spell. And the obeah worldview was a reality to Kincaid's mother as well: "She lived in a really spooky place where the things you saw were not real. You'd see lights in the mountains at night and it wasn't a star, it was a jablesse [a person who can turn into anything]. . . . [She] did have this experience I've written about, of throwing the stones at the monkey that one day caught the stone and threw it back at her" (Simmons).

Obeah practice occasionally touched the lives of Kincaid and her brothers. Once, after a schoolyard confrontation, the mother of a schoolmate threatened to put a spell on Kincaid so that she would drown herself. Kincaid was sent to stay with her grandmother on Dominica, since "crossing seawater is always a good way to get rid of a curse; the evil spirits couldn't follow"(Simmons).

In the world of obeah, Kincaid said, life is lived in the subconscious: "Instead of going for an hour on the couch, your entire life was on the couch, a world of nervous breakdowns." And while she "hated the whole thing," with all its secrets and secret relationships, at the same time, she seemed to lament what she sees as its passing: "Now the layer of obeah life doesn't work any more, doesn't exist any more. . . . I think it has to do with television . . . that world which turns out to have been quite rich is lost. So rich in your imagination, and imagination led to worlds" (Simmons).

The practice of obeah suggested a hidden reality behind visible reality; a similar effect was achieved by the imperial presence of England, which continued in Antigua through Kincaid's childhood. From the "Made in England" stamp on the box of breakfast cocoa, to the requirement on every school exam to "draw a map of England," to the brown felt hat her father wore, in imitation of an Englishman and in disregard for the climate, England was held up to the Caribbean child as the "real" reality, even if not quite visible from where she stood. In her essay "On Seeing England for the First Time," Kincaid wrote:

> I did not know then that the statement "Draw a map of England" was something far worse than a declaration of war, for a flat-out declaration of war would have put me on alert. In fact, there was no need for war—I had long ago been conquered. I did not know then that this statement was part of a process that would result in my erasure—not my physical erasure, but my erasure all the same. I did not know then that this statement was meant to make me feel awe and small whenever I heard the word "England": awe at the power of its existence, small because I was not from it.[18]

The children were drilled in English history, but this is not what had the greatest impact: "There were other views, subtler ones, softer, almost not there, but these softer views were the ones that made the most lasting impression on me, the ones that made me really feel like nothing" ("SE," 14). These could be conveyed through a phrase such as "when morning touched the sky" or "evening approaches," for "no morning touched the sky where I lived. The morning where I lived came on abruptly, with a shock of heat and loud noises. . . . Evenings where I lived did not approach; in fact, I had no evening—I had night and day, and they came and went in a mechanical way: on, off, on, off." The conclusion that a child drew from this contradiction was that "we must have done something to deserve" a world that so clearly was not what the world ought to be ("SE," 14).

Although the colonial education was clearly designed, as Kincaid now sees it, to "erase" the reality of the colonial child, this design was not commonly perceived. Kincaid's mother was at that time in her life, Kincaid says, an "Anglophile" who strove to give her daughter a "middle-class English upbringing" (Cudjoe, 400). Everyone around Kincaid seemed to accept English domination, and the doctrine that a thing could be "divine and good only if it was English" (Cudjoe, 398). Yet Kincaid could not help seeing the contradictions: "When I was nine, I refused to stand up at the refrain 'God Save Our King.' I hated 'Rule, Brittania'; and I used to say that we weren't Britons, we were slaves. I never had any idea why. I just thought that there was no sense to it" (Cudjoe, 397).

In *Annie John*, the young protagonist has a daydream in which she imagines herself "living alone in Belgium, a place I had picked when I read in one of my books that Charlotte Brontë, the author of my favorite novel, *Jane Eyre*, had spent a year or so there" (*AJ*, 92). Not only would going to Belgium allow Annie to emulate her writer-heroine, but Belgium was such a distant and unknown place that her mother would never be able to find her. In reality, the young Elaine Potter Richardson went neither to Belgium nor England, but took the short plane ride to America. Here, less in emulation of Brontë than Jane Eyre, she would trace the unlikely trajectory from servitude and obscurity to prominence and power.

Kincaid—still Richardson—first went to Scarsdale, New York, to work as a live-in baby-sitter. Her employers, according to the account in "Jamaica Kincaid's New York," were "very nice and protective" and amused about their young baby-sitter's fascination with New York City, 45 minutes away by train. Of herself at that period, Kincaid wrote,

> That was the first thing I wanted to do, take the train to New York. The first thing I did, though, I bought a girdle with a large red rose decorating the front paneling. I had never seen a girdle or known anyone who wore a girdle before. But from magazines and films, I had gathered that all up-to-date American women wore girdles. I, at the time, was 5'11" and weighed 107 pounds. Along with the girdle I bought a padded brassiere that made the nipples of my breasts look like newly sharpened pencils. Then I had my hair straightened with a cream for the first time

(before I had it pressed with a heated comb), and I had it styled in a way that made me look like the pictures of Negro American girls I had seen in *Tan* magazine. Of all the things I had wanted to be when I was little, being a Negro American girl like the girls in *Tan* magazine was one of the three that I was most serious about. The girls in *Tan* magazine looked to me to be tough and bad and worldly, and in my mind girls like that didn't live in Chicago or Detroit or Cincinnati. Girls like that lived in New York. ("JKNY," 71)

Soon Kincaid left Scarsdale to take another au pair job in New York City, this time, like the protagonist of *Lucy*, looking after four little girls of a well-to-do family. Also like Lucy, Kincaid became interested in photography, taking courses in photography at the New School for Social Research. Her mother, like the mother in *Annie John*, had intended that she study nursing. After leaving her au pair job, Kincaid, who had never been interested in nursing, went for a while to Franconia College in New Hampshire, but then returned to New York City, where she began a career in publishing:

[I] found a job with a magazine called *Art Direction*, I think. I was fired for writing an article on black American advertising. It was very controversial because I said something—I can't remember what it was—that made everyone upset, and so I was fired.

I thought I was entitled to unemployment insurance, but my unemployment checks never came, so I really had to try to find a job. I applied for a job at *Mademoiselle* and *Glamour*, but I couldn't type, so I didn't get these jobs. I submitted ideas to a magazine called *Ingenue*, and they didn't like any of them except one, in which I said I would like to ask Gloria Steinem what she was like when she was the age of the average reader of the magazine *Seventeen*. They thought that was a good idea and Gloria Steinem kindly granted me an interview, and I wrote the article.

It was a big success, and they turned it into a series of articles. They even sent me to Los Angeles to interview celebrities, asking them what they were like when they were seventeen. This was the first writing I did. (Cudjoe, 396)

It was around this time, in 1973, that 24-year-old Elaine Potter Richardson became Jamaica Kincaid. Kincaid has explained the change in numerous ways. It was a way of shucking family disapproval of her writing and of gaining a sort of anonymity: "This was a way to talk about things without people knowing it was me."[19] The choice of name was not particularly political, Kincaid told an interviewer:

At the time I changed it, I didn't know there were African names, although I don't think I could have done that because by this time I have as much connection to Africa as you do. The connection I have to Africa is the color of my skin and that doesn't seem enough to have changed it to an African name. My new name unconsciously had the significance I wanted it to have, since that is the area of the world I'm from. Jamaica is an English corruption of what Columbus called Xaymaca. Kincaid just seemed to go together with Jamaica, but there were many combinations of names that could have been chosen one night when my friends and I were sitting around. (Vorda, 15)

The renaming seems to have been the nearly instinctual act of someone who knows herself to be losing one self and finding another. Almost 20 years later, Kincaid put the act of renaming into a deeper context, seeing the "naming of things" as "crucial to possession. . . . It is not surprising that when people have felt themselves prey to [conquest], among the first acts of liberation is to change their names."[20]

Changing her name was not Kincaid's only act of liberation. She began, as she says, to "dress rather strangely. . . . I would wear a lot of old clothes, and sort of looked like people from different periods—someone from the 1920s, someone from the 1930s, someone from the 1940s. I had cut off all my hair and bleached it blond, and I had shaved off my eyebrows. I really did look odd" (Cudjoe, 397). Her friend George Trow, the *New Yorker* writer who gave Kincaid her introduction to the magazine, also remembers Kincaid's unconventional dress: "Jamaica wore jodhpurs. And her hair was dyed blond and cut very short. She would sometimes wear a tam-o'-shanter and a kind of red, red lipstick, a very vibrant lipstick. It was just as extreme a statement as a person could make that this was someone who did not necessarily fit anyone's conventional idea of who she should be" (Garis, 76).

For a young woman from a small place who "less than two years earlier . . . had been a schoolgirl in Antigua worrying about how much starch to put in my gray linen uniforms," New York City was a strange place. One aspect was particularly striking: "It was the way the people I met seemed free. I didn't know what they were free from, but I liked the way they moved about, and I liked the way they seemed happy and the way they seemed to come and go with no questions asked. I thought that I might like my life to be like that" ("JKNY," 72).

Still, in Kincaid's early journalism, one can detect a wariness under the bedazzlement, as if Kincaid is already sensing the dangers that may accompany a too successful transition to "another self." She describes the distaste she feels when people who have known her for "five seconds" tell her they love her; she behaves badly at parties, she says, so that she will not be asked back, fearing that she will like parties too much and become a "New York party goer" ("JKNY," 73). Kincaid's ambivalence about being taken up too suddenly by trendy New York society may be demonstrated by the picture that accompanies the *Rolling Stone* piece "Jamaica Kincaid's New York": a full page has been devoted to a photograph of the author, but all that is shown are her empty sandals, socks, blouse, hat, and a short skirt with a pack of Lucky Strikes tucked into the waistband, and of the author herself, only a thin naked forearm reaching toward the outfit, apparently holding a pen in her hand. In the caption, Kincaid noted that in obeah practice it is possible to kill someone by using a photograph of the person and that "someone has told me that this is the way South American Authorities display the clothing of South American guerrillas they have killed" ("JKNY," 71). With visibility comes an undercurrent of anxiety, the fear that if you become too visible, you might somehow be stolen from yourself.

We can also see Kincaid both fascinated and repulsed by her observations of what becomes of those who achieve fame and fortune, and in the light of Kincaid's subsequent rise to prominence, one wonders whether she was already studying how she herself might handle such a change. In this wariness of the well-to-do, there is again an echo of Kincaid's childhood heroine, Jane Eyre, the governess who goes among the wealthy and prominent but never allows herself to be made over as one of them. As Jane Eyre consistently disapproves of the fine, vapid ladies encountered in Edward Rochester's drawing room,[21] Kincaid, as she describes herself in *Rolling Stone*, takes care to insult a man who writes about "what rich writers are doing in the Hamptons" ("JKNY," 73).

In a 1976 review of a Diana Ross concert for the *Village Voice*, Kincaid considered the particular effects of success and prominence on a black woman, observing that Ross's success has come as a result of "devotion to imitation." There is here an inescapable sense of identification as Kincaid confides that Ross's voice on the recording "Baby Love" sounds "just the way I wanted to be. It was so cool, so sexy, so sweet, so pretty, all of those things for two-and-a-half minutes. . . . It was the voice of a young girl wanting everything yet not knowing what it was that she wanted or what it was that she would get."[22]

But, after noting Ross's numerous costume changes and the introduction of her "three half-white daughters," Kincaid makes this observation about her former idol, "Not only was she a young woman who conveyed the innocence of a girl, but she was a black person who had mastered without the slightest bit of self-consciousness or embarrassment, being white." Her voice has no "trace of anything relatively black," no church experience, no street experience, a kind of emptying-out that no Motown charm school could have accomplished. Ross, Kincaid suspected, "knew there was something awfully neat about a black person being white," and from this she generalizes, "There are two things a black girl can do and be really cool. She can be Bad. Or she can be White." This is a complex undertaking: "For a white person [to imitate black people] it becomes an exercise of the intellect resulting in maybe a parody, maybe a tribute. But for the black person who has the most to lose in terms of cultural identity it's deadly serious business. The approach is never one of serious study but a devotion to imitation." As a result, Kincaid does not much like anything Ross has done recently, as "all the things about her then that seemed fresh and innocent became hard and calculating"("Last," 150).

Twelve years later, Kincaid would take care to drop the "charm" that reviewers so loved in her most successful book, *Annie John*, declaring, "I've really come to love anger."[23] Almost 20 years later, Kincaid is still studying the question of the cultural identity of the black person who has been successful in the white world, wondering "at whose expense" she has "joined the conquering class" ("Flowers," 154).

There is a sense of magical, sudden recognition in Kincaid's account of how she was discovered by the New York literary establishment. Kincaid's impact on well-connected literary men reminds one of the impact the governess Jane Eyre has on the aristocratic Mr. Rochester when they first meet on a road. Upon first seeing the young girl, Rochester thinks she "has rather the look of another world" and considers asking whether she has "bewitched" his horse (Brontë, 153). Kincaid described her first encounter with literary New York thus:

One day, in the elevator, I met a man named Michael O'Donaghue. . . . This man seemed very taken by my appearance. He invited me to dinner and introduced me to a man named George W. S. Trow who wrote for the *New Yorker*. He and I became very good friends, and he used to write "The Talk of the Town" stories about me. One day he took me to dinner—I was very poor, so sometimes he'd take me to dinner. We were sitting in a Lebanese restaurant on 28th Street. I had just said something, and he said, "That's so funny! Would you like to write for the *New Yorker*? I should introduce you to Mr. Shawn."

I said, "Sure—of course. I'd love to write for the *New Yorker*." So he arranged for me to have lunch with Mr. Shawn at the Algonquin. Mr. Shawn said that I should try writing some "Talk" stories. I don't think anyone really thought I could do it—I mean, I know I didn't think so. Well, that's how I began to write for the *New Yorker*. (Cudjoe, 397)

Kincaid's first "Talk of the Town" piece—the first of some 80 such pieces spanning a decade—was published in September 1974. It contains Kincaid's remarks as she and a companion drive to a West Indian carnival held annually in Brooklyn. Though the subject of the piece is the carnival, Kincaid characteristically used the occasion to talk about her mother. Noting that what you do at Carnival is "jump up" when you get too excited to sit still, Kincaid confided, "I love to go to Carnival now, because when I was growing up my mother *would not let me 'jump up!'*"[24] Some of the subsequent "Talk of the Town" pieces are distinctly autobiographical, such as the 3 January 1983 piece about a West Indian carpenter-father. Others cover a wide variety of topics, from humorous tips on how to decorate a tiny apartment to make it seem bigger, to the observations of a Jamaican beauty contestant in Manhattan.

Four years later came another turning point when Kincaid, under the influence of the Elizabeth Bishop poem "In the Waiting Room" (Simmons), wrote the short story "Girl" in a single afternoon. The one-sentence story, filling a magazine page, would be her first *New Yorker* fiction and the first story in the collection *At the Bottom of the River*. The voice here is very different from that of Kincaid's journalism. The long, detailed lists that frequently mark the journalism are still there, along with the minute observation, but the slightly self-conscious tone of a smart, defiant, but careful schoolgirl has vanished, as has any conventional sense of story and direction. The voice now speaks to and for itself, as if in a dream or a deep reverie; the connections are those of the subconscious.

That afternoon, she knew that she had found her voice as a writer: "I somehow got more confident in what I knew about language. Finding your voice brings great confidence."[25] Not surprisingly, the voice Kincaid found is that of a mother, instructing and berating her young daughter. As Kincaid had come to realize, no matter how far from home she might go, no matter the changes she might make, she would never leave home and would never stop hearing her mother's voice. The freedom of New York, it seems, and the empowerment of success as a journalist allowed Kincaid not only to see that her mother is the "fertile soil" of her creative life (Cudjoe, 402) but also to dare finally to dig into that soil.

Kincaid's breakthrough was not only psychological. It was also the result of an examination of her basic assumptions about writing. A voracious reader as a child, she was well schooled in the classic works of English literature by the colonial system. So thoroughly was she taught the classics that she assumed all literature was created in the past, never imagining that people were still writing: "I thought that all the people who wrote seriously were dead. All the serious writers I read were dead from the nineteenth century back" (Simmons). As a result, Kincaid never thought of writing herself, nor did the premodernist storytelling mode she learned from the British works seem useful in exploring her own experience: in her world there was no reliable "realism," and things and people could never be trusted to be what they seemed to be. Further, Kincaid had come to believe that a directional narrative was almost never an attempt to tell a true story and almost always a way of lying about the world.

Two things changed Kincaid's thinking about writing. One was a French film called *La Jetée* made up of black-and-white still photographs, and the other was the work of the experimental French writer Alain Robbe-Grillet. Of the inspiration she received from Robbe-Grillet, Kincaid said:

> I never knew that the workings of your own mind, or that my own mind, would be interesting. [The Robbe-Grillet work] has no established form, no credentials, . . . that one could just do that, I was never the same after I read it, and I was never the same after I saw *La Jetée*. I just knew. I thought, "Oh, I see." Because I had grown up in this system in which . . . a straight line, you did this, and then if you passed that hurdle, you did that, and if you passed that hurdle you did that and then of course there was the final hurdle that you could never pass, you could never be English, you could never be a real person. So . . . no matter what you did, there would always be this incredible barrier. So then I read him, and saw this movie. . . . When I read that everything changed. (Simmons)

Through these French works, then, Kincaid seems to have seen a way of writing about her life and home without recourse to a storytelling mode she had come to see as archaic and dishonest. In her work, as in the black-and-white stills of *La Jetée* and the non-narrative scenes of Robbe-Grillet, both writer and reader are freed of the need to make conventionally coherent arrangements of experience and reality, and are invited instead to follow the author's chain of subliminal connections to find psychological, if not cognitive, sense.

At the same time, Kincaid has not jettisoned all aspects of her colonial education. Milton's *Paradise Lost*, for example, portions of which she was forced to memorize as punishment, gave her her first notion of what would become her own central theme, the relationship of the powerful to the powerless. Reading *Paradise Lost* and identifying with Lucifer "left with me this feeling of articulating your own pain, as Lucifer did. It seemed that if you couldn't say what was wrong with you, then you couldn't act. . . . I felt quite aggrieved as a child. . . . I did feel that I was cast out of my own paradise" (Simmons).

Although Kincaid sees writing as an act of liberation, she refused to claim membership in any literary "army." While she acknowledges that feminism has probably contributed to her success, she does not want to be categorized as a woman writer (Cudjoe, 401). Nor does she want to be categorized as a black writer: "It's just too slight to cling to your poor skin color or your sex . . . when you think of the great awe that you exist at all. The other stuff is too important to attach any importance to" (DeVries, 41–42). The simple fact of being black and female, Kincaid seems to say, does not necessarily cause people to share an identity. Of Zora Neale Hurston, she said, "I think that I do not appreciate her as some people do because I have not had a certain kind of experience. The language makes assumptions about things that I just don't understand" (Perry interview, 140). And while Kincaid "considers Toni Morrison one of the great writers of our time," she does not feel that she identifies personally with the African-American women Morrison writes about: "When I read about Black women's struggles here I obviously feel something. But not an identification. I would support it [the struggle], but I don't see myself in it. I have almost never identified myself with anybody else."[26] Kincaid was asked by *Essence* magazine whether her marriage to a white man represents a "contradiction." "'No, no, no,' Kincaid says with impatience. 'The marriage is a contradiction if you see the race and the person as one entity. There's a thing that goes on and there are the individuals who don't participate in it. . . . What you want to defeat is the idea that says your individuality doesn't count—that all you are is Black. You want to say, "But I'm a person. Not a political entity""" (Edwards, 90).

Kincaid refuses to see herself as a "political entity," but she also believes people must keep their "history" in mind. Kincaid is careful not to appear to be in any way minimizing the domination experienced by those with a slave and colonial heritage or to be distancing herself from it:

> There was an attempt, successful, by English colonization to make a certain kind of person out of me, and it was a success, it worked, it really worked. My history of domination, culturally, in all the ways it existed is true. It was a success. I do not spend my present time trying to undo it. I do not, for instance, spend my life now attempting to have some true African heritage. My history is that I came from African people who were enslaved and dominated by European, British people and that is it. And there is no attempt to erase it. (Simmons)

By 1983, 17 years after leaving Antigua to work as a baby-sitter, Jamaica Kincaid was a literary star. Her first book, *At the Bottom of the River*, a collection of ten *New Yorker* stories, including the breakthrough story "Girl," won the Morton Dauwen Zabel Award of the American Academy and Institute of Arts and Letters, was nominated for the PEN/Faulkner Award, and was widely reviewed by critics who were often adulatory and always respectful, even when puzzled by the surreal nature of the book. Kincaid was heralded by such preeminent literary figures as Susan Sontag, who wrote that at least two of the stories, "My Mother" and "At the Bottom of the River," "seem to me more thrilling than any prose I've read in the last few years by a writer from this continent."[27] And Derek Walcott said he read the book with "that soft succession of 'yeses' that we silently give to what Hemingway called 'the true sentence.'"[28]

Two years later, there appeared the more accessible *Annie John,* also originally published as short stories in the *New Yorker*. The book was one of three finalists for the 1985 international Ritz Paris Hemingway Award, and this time the reviews were almost universally laudatory: "Rarely has so much been done in so few pages."[29] "Her language recalls Henri Rousseau's painting: seemingly natural, but in reality sophisticated and precise" (Austin, 7).

Not only had Kincaid arrived in literary terms, but she had begun to form a new family. In 1979 she married the composer Allen Shawn, son of William Shawn, the *New Yorker* editor. By 1985 she had a baby daughter, Annie, and three years later, the couple had a son, Harold. Rather than seeing a family as a hindrance to writing, Kincaid sees it as an almost necessary condition. Speaking from her home in North Bennington, Vermont, where her husband is a faculty member at Bennington College, she told interviewer Donna Perry,

I think I have to have a great deal of activity to write. I am essentially a person very interested in domestic life and very interested in things that we think of, either in a good way or a bad way, as women's things. I know a woman and she comes to see me in the morning and we sit at the kitchen table. We just sit and talk. That's not how I write but in a way it is. . . . In fact, I think I reduce everything to a domestic situation. . . . It's not anything deliberate or a statement or anything, that's just how I understand things. (Perry interview, 136–37)

But if Kincaid has written herself into literary success, she has also, through writing, come to "discover [her] own mind," and one thing she has discovered in it seems to be a great deal of anger. Kincaid feels she reached a "turning point" in the writing of the long essay *A Small Place*. The essay was written

with a kind of recklessness. . . . I didn't know what I would say ahead of time. Once I wrote it I felt very radicalized by it. I would have just thought of myself as a liberal person until I wrote it, and now I feel that liberal is as far right as I can go . . . . I've really come to love anger. And I liked it even more when a lot of reviews said it's so angry. The *New York Times* said that the book didn't have the "charm" of *Annie John*. Really, when people say you're charming you are in deep trouble. I realized in writing that book that the first step to claiming yourself is anger. (Perry interview, 132–33)

A Small Place was written for the *New Yorker*'s William Shawn, who liked it, Kincaid said, but it was rejected as too angry by Robert Gottlieb, the editor who had replaced Shawn. It was then published in book form in 1988, and certainly no one called it charming. Nor did reviewers miss the anger. Salman Rushdie described it as "a jeremiad of great clarity and a force that one might have called torrential were the language not so finely controlled."[30] Many reviewers, such as Michiko Kakutani of the *New York Times*, did not find the anger at "Europeans and North Americans who routinely patronized and humiliated the Antiguans" misplaced; Kakutani also noted that Kincaid's "observations concerning contemporary, self-ruled Antigua . . . tend to be just as unsparing as her assessments of its colonial condition."[31] But another reviewer for the *New York Times* asserted that the book was "distorted by [Kincaid's] anger."[32] And a reviewer for the British journal *New Statesman and Society* appears to have been himself infuriated by the book: "Unfortunately the author quickly loses control of her material, and inexplicably descends into a sniveling attack on the sins of the nasty—and long-departed—colonial power."[33]

Despite the disagreement over *A Small Place*, the *New Yorker* continued to publish Kincaid's fiction, and in 1990 five stories were collected and published as the novel *Lucy*. While *Lucy* contains little of the overt political anger of *A Small Place*, it is still a work obsessed by the question of how domination hinders the formation of authentic identity. The stories take up where *Annie John* left off, showing the further progress of a young West Indian girl who leaves her mesmerizing mother and her Caribbean home, going out to conquer her own version of the New World. In *Lucy*, the title character works as a baby-sitter for a white family. Beautiful and wealthy, the family seems to present a portrait of perfection until the X-ray vision of the young girl reveals a turmoil that will soon break the family apart.

Some reviewers were disappointed with the book. Writing in the *New York Times Book Review*, Thulani Davis found it "difficult to recognize the lively, curious and engaged child Annie in the angry but disengaged Lucy."[34] Jane Mendelsohn, however, saw that "with its subtle evocation of shifting patterns, *Lucy* reveals more gradations in the quality of possible experience than any of Kincaid's previous books."[35]

With *Lucy*, as with all of Kincaid's work, it is impossible to separate fiction from life, and the book "upset some of Kincaid's friends and colleagues," apparently because the wealthy, troubled family in the book closely parallels that of the writer Michael Arlen, who employed Kincaid in real life and later became her colleague at the *New Yorker*. Of the complaint that Kincaid has used her former acquaintances and colleagues, Kincaid told an interviewer that "the only person in the book who is drawn directly from life is Lucy, the title character. The others are composites." But, Kincaid adds, "I would never say I wouldn't write about an experience I've had" (Garis, 78).

Kincaid's most recent work of fiction, "The Autobiography of My Mother" ("But it's not that," she said [Simmons]) is set in the West Indies and narrated by the same young woman who tells Kincaid's story "Song of Roland." This latter story, published in the *New Yorker* in the spring of 1993, was the first of Kincaid's fiction to explore the West Indies from an adult's point of view, rather than a child's. The Roland of the title is a stevedore for whom the narrator develops a passion: "I bathed my face then between his legs; he smelt of curry and onions, for those were the things he had been unloading all day; other times when I bathed my face between his legs—for I did it often, I liked doing it—he would smell of sugar, or flour, or the large, cheap bolts of cotton from which he would steal a few yards to give me to make a dress." Since

Roland is married, the narrator also comes to know his wife, for, says the narrator, "I could not have loved Roland the way I did if he had not loved other women."[36]

In her recent nonfiction, Kincaid has continued to explore the question of "domination" and the relationship between the powerful and the powerless. In the bitter essay "On Seeing England for the First Time," Kincaid, as noted earlier, wrote of her childhood, in which "England was to be our source of myth and the source from which we got our sense of reality, our sense of what was meaningful, our sense of what was meaningless" ("SE," 13). The children were so imbued with an idea of England, Kincaid wrote, that a large space inevitably opened up between that idea and the reality of England. For Kincaid, the space "had become filled with hatred and so when at last I saw [England] I wanted to take it into my hands and tear it into little pieces" ("SE," 16). Since she could not do that, she could only "indulge in not-favorable opinions," and so she finds everything about England ugly and smelly. She understands that she may be "prejudiced," but she also recognizes to her despair that her prejudice cannot have the same impact upon the English as their prejudice had upon her: "My prejudices have no weight to them, my prejudices have no force behind them, my prejudices remain opinions, my prejudices remain my personal opinion. And a great feeling of rage and disappointment came over me as I looked at England, my head full of personal opinions that could not have public, my public, approval. The people I come from are powerless to do evil on a grand scale" ("SE," 16).

Kincaid's most recent examination of the theme of domination has come in the form of an occasional column for the *New Yorker* called "In the Garden." A gardener at her home in Vermont, Kincaid has come to see writing about gardening as the "perfect way of writing about domination," saying, "I don't know how anyone avoided it" (Simmons).

One theme of Kincaid's gardening columns is the way in which plants have historically been seized as part of the treasure of conquest, how they have been taken from their native environments, renamed, and then transplanted in a new land. Sometimes the plants are used to enrich the new land, sometimes to beautify, sometimes to replace the failing indigenous flora. For Kincaid, this gathering, renaming, and transplanting is a form of, and metaphor for, conquest. The "cocoxochitl" is taken from Mexico and Central America to Europe, for example, and "hybridized by the Swedish botanist Andreas Dahl," who renames the plant after himself. Thereafter, the "dahlia" becomes a European possession losing all connection to its native Central America ("Flowers," 155).

Like the child who could not understand why everyone around her so mindlessly sang "Rule, Brittania," Kincaid cannot understand why no one else seems to be thinking about this type of conquest. She is shocked when she reads biographies of "plant hunters, or botanists, what I call thieves," to see that no one else apparently sees such gathering and transplanting as a kind of conquest, as first stealing from the native peoples and then seeking to erase the crime by changing the name. The accounts of the exploits of European botanists are "heartbreaking," "a kind of spiritual genocide" (Simmons).

If the gardening column, which Kincaid expects to continue and to publish in collected form, is about domination, it is also very much about Kincaid herself, a continuation of the autobiographical project. In it, we find a theme that began to surface in Kincaid's earliest journalism, the uneasiness of the once-disempowered person who, rather suddenly, finds herself becoming part of what she herself terms "the conquering class" ("Flowers," 159). As she considers her own garden, Kincaid notices that she has joined a group for whom the work of growing plants is a pleasure rather than a backbreaking necessity. Gardening, as Kincaid does it now, is a luxury of the conqueror, one that, moreover, cruelly imitates the toil of the conquered:

> There was a day not long ago when I realized with a certain amount of bitterness that I was in my garden, a flower garden, a garden planted only because I wished to have such a thing, and that I knew how I wanted it to look and knew the name, proper and common, of each thing growing in it. In the place I am from, I would have been a picture of shame: a woman covered with dirt, smelling of manure, her hair flecked with white dust (powdered lime), her body a cauldron of smells pleasing to her, her back crooked with pain from bending over. ("Flowers," 158)

Even in success, the sense of irreplaceable loss and mysterious, hidden betrayal that has permeated Kincaid's work is not wiped away. "I had crossed a line; but at whose expense? I cannot begin to look, because what if it is someone I know?" ("Flowers," 159).

Chapter Two

Mother Mystery

In Kincaid's three works of fiction a crisis of loss centers on the mother, and any consideration of Kincaid's writing must begin with an examination of this theme. Not only is the rift between mother and daughter central, but this agony of division can also be seen as a metaphor for another primary theme that emerges in Kincaid's later work, racial or cultural domination.

In *Annie John* the importance of the break between mother and daughter is unmistakable; without warning, the adored and adoring mother turns on her daughter. The mother is suddenly distant, angry, and critical, and the daughter, for whom her mother has been the world, is devastated. In *At the Bottom of the River* this rupture is not portrayed so explicitly; rather, it is a black thread running through a kaleidoscope of dreamlike images. While in *Annie John* we see a loving and beloved mother turn into a cold, sometimes hated figure, in *At the Bottom of the River* we see the beautiful mother turn effortlessly into a serpent with spinning, blazing eyes. In *Lucy*, Kincaid's protagonist physically escapes her mother by leaving her Caribbean home, and for a time her struggle to survive in a new world seems to take precedence over the struggle to free herself from the paralyzing pain of losing the mother's love. But once Lucy finds her footing in the new setting, the powerful presence of the mother, "a ball of fury, large, like a god," planted in Lucy's psyche, makes its presence known (*Lucy*, 150).

Kincaid gives us again and again the daughter's inner turmoil, her longing, her rage, and the sense that the profundity of the loss has "erased" her (*BR*, 47). The cause of this rupture between the mutually adoring mother and daughter is never fully explained, remaining a mystery at the heart of Kincaid's work. In Kincaid's first work of fiction, *At the Bottom of the River*, the mother's transformation from woman to serpent seems to be the result of some evil magic that no one, not even the mother herself, entirely understands. In *Annie John* the rift between mother and daughter is clearly linked to the girl's approaching puberty; it is only after the 12-year-old Annie suddenly grows tall and gangly and discovers "small tufts of hair . . . under [her] arms" (*AJ*, 25) that the mother, in Annie's view, suddenly turns on her. Still, the ferocity of the conflict between mother and daughter seems to go well beyond the usual trauma that puberty causes in mother and child.

In *Lucy*, Kincaid's protagonist gets a glimpse of the mother as flawed personality, someone who could never get beyond her own need to control and so would never see that sometimes her child's "needs were more important than her wishes"(*Lucy*, 64). Although Lucy comes to this insight, she still cannot get a clear fix on her mother, who continues to be frighteningly changeable—sometimes the lost love of Lucy's life, sometimes the very devil. Describing her mother in terms of romantic passion, Lucy says, "I had been mourning the end of a love affair, perhaps the only true love in my whole life I would ever know" (*Lucy*, 132). Casting her mother as a devil, she compares herself with a girl who escapes an abusive, devil-possessed parent by crossing the ocean "because the Devil cannot walk over water" (*Lucy*, 21).

As Kincaid talks of her own mother, one senses that she, too, remains a painful mystery. Interviewed after *Lucy* was published, Kincaid noted that she lost her position as only child at the age of nine when the first of three brothers was born, and one might speculate that this could be enough to plunge a sensitive child into the crisis of loss examined in Kincaid's fiction. But the author believes there was something more, some inexplicable "withdrawal of affection" (Garis, 70).

Increasingly interested in questions of domination, Kincaid has come to see her mother as a victim of a colonial and racist system, a woman "ultimately defeated" by the requirement that she internalize the conflict between two worldviews. Kincaid sees that this may have a direct impact on the mother-daughter relationship. Having internalized the notion that a rampant sensuality is inherent to people of African heritage, for example, her mother saw "any sensuality as just the end," Kincaid says. And it was necessary for the mother to see her maturing daughter in this light: "My mother really said, 'You've turned into a slut,' when she went out of control. The slut thing was not advice. It was a wish" (Simmons).

Still, no explanation extinguishes the hope Kincaid seems to nourish for a common ground with her mother, even if it is only a shared past. But this hope soon vanishes, miragelike, as Kincaid gets close to it. When she sees her mother now, Kincaid tries to get her to remember aspects of their life together. Her mother, however, refuses; she is not, Kincaid says, "interested in memory at all" (Simmons).

The mysterious catastrophe of lost love at the center of Kincaid's work may be examined with the help of two studies that explore the psychology of mother-daughter relationships. The sudden emotional abandonment of a previously beloved child is common in the world of psychologist Alice Miller's narcissistic mothers, those whose sense of self is inadequate and who use their children for their own emotional requirements, needing "someone at their disposal who can be used as an echo, who can be controlled, is completely centered on them, will never desert them, and offers full attention and admiration."[1] The narcissistic parent approves of the child fully as long as the child focuses all of his or her love and attention on the parent. But any move toward maturity or autonomy on the part of the child is experienced by the parent as a hostile act, even as an attack, and the parent responds with a combination of hurt and anger (Miller, 33).

Thus, in *Annie John* the mother who has previously spent whole afternoons sorting lovingly through a trunk containing Annie's childhood memorabilia suddenly refuses Annie's request to look at the trunk: "A person I did not recognize answered in a voice I did not recognize, 'Absolutely not! You and I don't have time for that anymore'"(*AJ*, 27). "Anymore" seems to be the present in which the 12-year-old girl has begun to show signs of impending maturity; Annie's mother can be seen as experiencing the "narcissistic rage" that results when "the object does not behave as we expect or wish" (Miller, 31), that is, when signs of developing a separate identity appear in the person one has counted on to reflect one back to oneself selflessly and constantly.

In *Lucy*, Kincaid's protagonist seems to have come to recognize the mother's narcissistic needs and how these govern her relations with her daughter: "I had come to feel that my mother's love for me was designed solely to make me into an echo of her. . . . Those thoughts would have come as a complete surprise to my mother, for in her life she had found that her ways were the best ways to have, and she would have been mystified as to how someone who came from inside her would want to be anyone different from her" (*Lucy*, 36).

While Alice Miller presents parental narcissism as a problem of personal psychology, Nancy Chodorow sees the root of maternal narcissism in family structures. Like Miller, Chodorow writes of mothers who do "not allow their daughters to perceive themselves as separate people" but act as if their daughters were "narcissistic extensions or doubles of themselves."[2] Chodorow sees this phenomenon as occurring particularly in patriarchal Western middle-class cultures in which a woman does not work outside the home, the extended family is fragmented, and a woman's only socially valued role is to raise her children, with whom she is isolated most of the time. It is not, Chodorow wrote, "surprising, then that she is likely to invest a lot of anxious energy and guilt in her concern for her children and to look to them for her own self-affirmation, or that her self-esteem, dependent on the lives of others than herself, is shaky. Her life situation leads her to an overinvolvement in her children's lives" (64). Such women are likely to suffer "boundary confusion," uncertainty over where they stop and another person begins (59). Further, "a mother is more likely to suffer this 'boundary confusion' with a daughter than with a son, to experience her daughter (or parts of her daughter's life) as herself" (47). Thus, these mothers "perpetuate a mutual relationship with their daughters of both primary identification and infantile dependence" (48). The mother is not able to encourage the daughter, whom she identifies in part as herself, to move toward a healthy separation. The daughter, for her part, may try to separate, but having been taught for so long to see herself as a part of her mother, often finds only an artificial and temporary method of establishing boundaries by "project[ing] what she defines as bad within her onto her mother and try[ing] to take what is good into herself" (59). This effort does not work to free the daughter. So bound is she to the mother that "conscious rejection of her oedipal maternal identification . . . remains an unconscious rejection and devaluation of herself" (65).

If we can see Miller's narcissistic mother in Kincaid's work, we may also detect, particularly in *At the Bottom of the River*, the daughter described by Chodorow, caught in infantile dependence, unable to find a healthy way to separate from the mother. In Kincaid's vision of the fiendishly transmuting mother, the lovely woman who turns into a serpent, we may see a daughter who is projecting what she fears is bad within herself onto her mother. The vision of the mother effortlessly metamorphosing herself into a serpent, for example, may be in part a projection of the daughter's guilty sense of her own "badness" for having evolved into a separate identity from her mother and for having entered, however involuntarily, the stage of puberty that inevitably causes some separation between mother and daughter.

If the Miller and Chodorow discussions tell us something about the mother as seen in Kincaid's fiction, they may also tell us something about the daughter, showing both women to be experiencing boundary confusion, both, on some level, suffering from a failure to establish a firm sense of self, one that does not rely extensively on a relationship with the other to exist. Each is furious at the other for not being able to continue the perfect union of mother and infant past puberty and into eternity. As the mother would hold the daughter, so would the daughter hold the mother. The daughter in Kincaid's fiction, especially in the surreal *At the Bottom of the River*, alternates between vivid visions of the evil, changing, betraying mother and equally vivid visions of mother and daughter joined in infantile bliss.

While the daughter's agony of loss, yearning, and rage at the mother often seems to dominate Kincaid's work, another mother-daughter theme is present in all of her fiction. In each of her three works of fiction, Kincaid's young protagonist, nearly destroyed by her struggles with her mother, turns to a substitute mother figure. In all three works, the relationship to this mother figure allows Kincaid's protagonist to keep moving forward toward her own separate identity. This other figure not only nurtures and heals the girl but also helps her to discover her own identity.

This figure corresponds to the "othermother" of African-American communities described by Patricia Hill Collins.[3] "Othermothers" are women who "assist bloodmothers by sharing mothering responsibilities" and who have "traditionally . . . been central to the institution of Black motherhood" (5).

Collins draws motherhood and its relation to society rather differently from Chodorow, a difference that has been related to that between capitalist and tribal societies.[4] Children are seen as the communal responsibility of a tribal society, it is argued. In middle-class Western society, by contrast, "motherhood is largely about private property: the children are the property of the father who 'loans' them temporarily to the mother, whose duty it is to raise those children according to the father's law."[5]

For Kincaid, writing out of a combined heritage of European colonialism and African tribalism, both visions of motherhood are present. Her childhood world is dominated not only by the colonial presence but also by a mother desperate, first, to turn the child into the kind of commodity—a "young lady"—that will meet with patriarchal approval and, then, to cling to that commodity as the only value her life has produced. Patriarchal ownership of the child is especially alienating for the mother, since the "patriarch" is not the biological father or even a male establishment that represents him but, rather, colonial power. This power usurps any role the biological father might play in the child's life.

While the colonial presence is central, it is not the only seat of power. As the mothers in all of Kincaid's fiction have not lost the ability to draw on obeah magic at times of great need, so Kincaid's protagonists have not lost the ability to draw on an ancient communal idea when all else fails. So, when the biological mother, nearly crazed by her desire to dominate and possess, fails her daughter, the girl is able to conjure up a magical othermother to help her find her way.

In *At the Bottom of the River*, the othermother theme is nearly impossible to detect without the clues provided by Kincaid's other works. In the collection's penultimate piece, "My Mother," the young protagonist, worn out by grief and anger, sleeps "the only dreamless sleep I ever had" and, upon waking, is taken to a jetty and put on a boat by her mother. Though the girl leaves her mother, she is greeted, when the boat reaches land again, by a woman she "recognizes" as her mother. It is a meeting of calm joy. The girl fits "perfectly in the crook of [the] mother's arm, on the curve of her back, in the hollow of her stomach. . . . We merge and separate, merge and separate; soon we shall enter the final stage of our evolution" (*BR*, 59–60). It is easy to see this episode as yet another fantasy of infantile union with the mother. On one level it surely is. But when viewed in terms of Kincaid's later work, what also seems apparent is that the peace achieved here—one that is not immediately dashed, as are most visions of harmony with the mother—is not in fact found with the mother but with a substitute.

The journey from an angry, rejecting mother to a calm, accepting maternal surrogate is foreshadowed in one of Kincaid's first published pieces of fiction, the 1978 story "Antigua Crossings." Here a girl who has angered her mother is sent on a ship from Antigua, where she lives, to stay with her maternal grandmother in Dominica. Like the girl in *At the Bottom of the River*, then, she leaves one mother and, after a sea voyage, finds another. The grandmother she finds is an imposing figure, a Carib Indian, "taller than her two daughters and . . . much blacker skinned than any black skinned person I have ever seen" (50). Unlike the mother left behind, the grandmother does not want anything from the girl or to blame her for anything. Rather, the grandmother is seen as a model of strength and serenity, a woman who knows exactly who she is. She is a figure to be respected and emulated instead of adored in a suffocating embrace:

At the end of every day, just before the sun sets completely, my grandmother sits on a little bench in front of her house and stares out at the

sea. She sits there and she stares and stares and says nothing at all to anyone. . . . My grandmother is a Christian now and she goes to church reg-
ularly but all of this is just to please her husband who is a lay minister in
the Methodist church. I have seen the way she hunts agouti and I know
that she has not forgotten the history of her ancestors and it makes me
glad. (48)

In *Annie John* this movement from the mother to the othermother is
clear, as the daughter, after a particularly painful exchange with her
mother, enters a deep sickness in which the world seems to go black.
This crisis is described as "a black thing . . . lying down [inside my
head], and it shut out all my memory of things that had happened to
me" (*AJ*, 111–12). Many efforts are made to cure the girl but to no avail.
Then, magically, as if in a fever dream, the girl's maternal grandmother
Ma Chess arrives and rescues the girl through remothering and even
rebirth: "I would lie on my side, curled up like a little comma, and Ma
Chess would lie next to me, curled up like a bigger comma, into which I
fit. . . . Ma Chess fed me my food, coaxing me to take mouthful after
mouthful. She bathed me and changed my clothes and sheets and did all
the other things that my mother used to do" (*AJ*, 126). When the girl is
cured, Ma Chess simply disappears, and Annie is free to take the next
step, which is to leave her mother and her home in search of a new life.
   In *Lucy* a very different othermother appears in the person of Mariah,
Lucy's rich white employer. Here Kincaid signals clearly that Mariah is
functioning as a mother figure and that Lucy is using this woman to sort
out the parts of her own mother that are healthy for her and the parts
that are detrimental: "The times that I loved Mariah it was because she
reminded me of my mother. The times that I did not love Mariah it was
because she reminded me of my mother" (58). Mariah has the mother's
serenity as she works in the kitchen, and the same large, expressive
hands. Mariah wants to control Lucy's life, as did the mother. Her disapproval of Lucy's new friends echoes the mother's attitudes. But there is a
difference. Mariah finally acknowledges that Lucy needs friends, however distasteful they may appear, and Lucy remarks, "This was a way in
which Mariah was superior to my mother" (63).
   In many ways, Lucy's naive white employer does not at all resemble
the previous othermothers. She is not an imposing, self-knowing figure
like the grandmother in "Antigua Crossings"; she does not induce a
dream of peaceful "merging and separating" like the figure in *At the
Bottom of the River*; she does not remother and rebirth the girl like Ma

Chess in *Annie John*. The most striking difference is that she lacks the omnipotence of these other characters, and this lack seems essential to the role Kincaid now needs the othermother to play. It seems Kincaid is finally able to imagine a mother figure who can offer affection and sympathy but is only human, incapable of superhuman understanding or control. Thus, Mariah is loving toward the young girl and tries to help her with information, but she is no fount of magical female power.

Mariah is hurt when Lucy decides to leave her and belatedly tries to institute a servant-master relationship. We can detect here an echo of the rupture between Annie and her mother as Mariah suddenly tries to switch from a relationship based on mutual affection to one based on power. However, in Mariah we see not a reflection of the mother Lucy has but of the one Lucy needs at this particular time. Mariah's displeasure has no great power over Lucy, who is only saddened to see Mariah trying to act like a master, knowing that it is "always hard for the person who is left behind" (141). Suddenly we grasp, as Lucy seems to grasp, that a grievous sense of abandonment may be part of what is behind the mother's vengeful fury: she is being left behind by a daughter who is not only maturing physically but will have to leave her island home to achieve her full growth. Finally, Lucy is able to see a maternal figure as just another individual with her own needs, rather than as an essential and omnipotent force. When Mariah gives her a cold farewell, Lucy does not take it "personally; someday we would be friends again," she says, and soon they are (*Lucy*, 144).

Thus, with Mariah, as with all the othermothers, Kincaid's protagonist is able to make another step toward her own healthy independence. With Mariah, Lucy replays her experience of leaving her own mother, but this time she does so calmly, knowing that the world does not explode when two people have differing desires, that her life is finally her own. She sees that it may even be possible to be reconciled one day with the person who has tried to keep you from yourself.

As noted earlier, the mother in Kincaid's fiction lives in a world of conflicting cosmologies. She seems, indeed, to have internalized two worldviews, that of British imperialism and that of African tribal custom and folk magic. As a result, she presents her child with an impossibly contradictory map of the world, and the daughter cannot hope to follow the mother's directions. To survive, the daughter must ignore the instructions that result from the mother's internalized contradictions; against the mother's ferocious resistance, she must seek to emulate the aspect of her mother that is still centered and powerful.

As the child in both *At the Bottom of the River* and *Annie John* approaches puberty, the mother increasingly imitates the colonial educational system, which seems bent on erasing all that is native to the child, rewarding only that which imitates the European rulers. Thus, the mother suddenly institutes a number of programs to make a young lady out of Annie; the girl is even sent for instruction in how to curtsy. But, just as the teachers in Annie's school constantly imply the basic inferiority of their students by holding up to them a model they will never be able to imitate, the mother constantly implies that the daughter's fundamental nature will always be that of a slut rather than of a young lady. Both teachers and mother repeat the subtle yet constant colonial theme: ceaseless effort must be made to civilize the child, to turn her into a satisfactory imitation of a European; this effort, though, can never be completely successful.

While the mother in Kincaid's work unquestionably joins with the colonial powers in trying to turn her daughter into a version of a middle-class English girl, this effort is not the only outlet for her energies, and in the mother's other activities, we detect the shape of a very different worldview. Although the engine of empire drives official and public life on the Caribbean island Kincaid portrays, life on the domestic level is in many ways running on an entirely different track. Here—except when the mother grows obsessed by what Annie calls "this young lady business" (*AJ*, 27)—there is no evidence of empire, the English, or, to a large extent, even men. The only man to intrude in any serious way is the mother's father, as seen in *Annie John*, with whom the mother quarrels over "whether she would live alone, as she wished, or would continue to live in her parents' house as her father wished" (*AJ*, 105). Even he is disposed of before the book begins, for Annie senior settled the quarrel by packing her things and leaving her father's house in Dominica for Antigua. The world she has created for herself on the new island is female, the concerns are domestic, and the power that really counts is a mix of housekeeping wisdom, folk remedies, and a reliance on the African-based obeah magic.

Even after she steps up her campaign to turn the girl into a young lady, as Helen Pyne Timothy noted, the mother in *Annie John* readily forsakes the European for the African worldview when real problems arise. Then she "falls back on the belief in folk wisdom, myth, African systems of healing and bush medicine, the mysteries of good and evil spirits inhabiting the perceived world of nature."[6] The same mother who in *At the Bottom of the River* instructs the girl not to "sing benna [African folk songs] in Sunday school" (3) only a few lines later articulates an outlook rather different from the one the girl will hear in Sunday school: "Don't pick people's flowers—you might catch something; don't throw stones at blackbirds, because it might not be a blackbird at all" (5).

On one level, then, the mother in Kincaid's fiction seems to have internalized racist and paternalistic colonial values. Her determination to make the child into something she cannot be, her support of a system that denies her own validity as much as it does the child's, seems to reflect her own sense of powerlessness and her desire to keep her daughter powerless. On another level, however, the mother presents the daughter with an unmistakable model of African-based female power, that of the obeah woman—one who can follow the shifting nature of reality, who can see through disguises, who can move swiftly to thwart evil forces and protect her own, who boldly decides what she wants and moves to get it. Though she seems to support colonial values, to the detriment of herself and her child, on some level she is a woman who always knows who she is and where her power lies.

The mother seems to want to weaken the girl. At the same time, she also offers her a model of female empowerment, an empowerment that extends far beyond the mother-daughter relationship. Not only is the mother herself powerful, but in *Annie John* her consultation with other women who practice obeah suggests the presence of a community of women who are able to read and control events. This community finally saves Kincaid's young protagonists. When the daughter's conflict with the mother grows too painful, triggering the emotional and physical breakdown seen in both *At the Bottom of the River* and *Annie John*, the girl is able to turn to another maternal figure without completely rejecting her actual mother, turning to a woman who represents her mother's power rather than her narcissism. This is seen most clearly in *Annie John*, where the substitute mother, the maternal grandmother Ma Chess, is a celebration of non-European, magical feminine power. In her, Timothy wrote, "Kincaid has provided a portmanteau figure of African myth and reality: Ma Chess is African healer, bush medicine specialist, and Caribbean obeah woman, extremely conscious of the presence of good and evil in life and able to ward off evil. She is also the mythological 'flying African' able to cross the seas without a boat and the flying 'soucouyant' (female witch)" (241). Ma Chess, like Annie's mother, has been exposed to European ways but has found them to be unworthy of imitation. Similarly, the "modern" practices of Annie's family do not impress her: "Ma Chess once asked my father to tell her exactly what it was he really did, and when he said he was off to build a house she said, 'A house? Why live in a house? All you need is a nice hole in the ground so you can come and go as you please'" (*AJ*, 126).

The othermother who finally helps the girl to "emerge" from her "pit" in *At the Bottom of the River* is, like Ma Chess, at home in an entirely magical realm, where she is effortlessly and invisibly in control: "The fishermen are coming in from sea; their catch is bountiful, my mother has seen to that" (60). Safe with this new mother, the girl, unconflicted, at least for the moment, can assume her own magical female powers: "A hummingbird has nested on my stomach, a sign of my fertileness" (61).

By *Lucy*, Kincaid's protagonist has incorporated much of her mother's strength into herself. Though she is in some ways still a confused child, she has attained her mother's power of vision. The mother in each of Kincaid's works is never deceived by appearances. She operates on the premise that reality is changeable and tricky, that form is not to be trusted, that nothing is entirely what it purports to be. Now Lucy seems to have acquired the same power. Effortlessly, she sees behind the masks of pretense and denial worn by the wealthy family for whom she works. And she is not fooled by the pleasing masks donned by colonial power to trick and manipulate its subjects. The beautiful and innocent form of the daffodil, for example, no longer masks the fact that by glorifying the daffodil in poetry and by ignoring Caribbean flora, colonial education has used the daffodil as a tool to "erase" everything that is native to the colonial child. Just as the mother in *At the Bottom of the River* knows that a blackbird "might not be a blackbird at all" (5), so Lucy, coming into her own powers of vision, can see that a daffodil may not be a daffodil but a weapon, part of "a scene of conquered and conquests" (*Lucy*, 30).

While Lucy continues to yearn for her powerful, magical mother, she no longer needs her as intensely as before. Although it has been a battle almost to the death, Kincaid's young protagonist—as we trace her progress through these three works—has overcome the debilitating message of the narcissistic, subjugated aspect of her mother. She still *is*, as she says in *Lucy*, her mother. But now she has discovered the mother's other aspect, the fierce, sure vision of the obeah woman.

Chapter Three
Conjure Woman

When Jamaica Kincaid's first book, *At the Bottom of the River*, appeared in 1983 it was widely praised for its poetic sensibility, its "care for language, joy in the sheer sound of words, and evocative power" (Tyler, 33). The very sound of the stories fascinated readers who found it "hypnotic," as if Kincaid were "magically chanting out bits of the subconscious" (Austin, 7). But the book also left some critics confused and even a little annoyed at their inability to understand quite what Kincaid was getting at. The stories are "almost insultingly obscure," Anne Tyler wrote, "and often fail to pull us forward with any semblance of a plot"(33). Another critic, writing in the *New York Times*, saw the pieces as "a literary equivalent of Rock video in which technical adroitness in manipulating an image and a sensuous pleasure in what can be done with it rather preclude questions about why."[1]

While the shifting realities and identities of *At the Bottom of the River* may at first seem too obscure to follow, a closer examination of the assumptions of Kincaid's Caribbean world suggests that this very fluidity of reality is the book's theme. Any discussion of the obscurity of Kincaid's work, especially *At the Bottom of the River*, must begin with an examination of the assumption that a particular kind of power exists in the world, obeah, the magical power of transformation.

Obeah, also known as conjure and voodoo, is described as the "transatlantic religion of diasporic and Afro-American masses in the New World," which is "descended from *voudun*, an African religion in which the priestess holds supreme power."[2] Conjure, Houston A. Baker, Jr., wrote, is about transformation, the power to "cause definitions of 'form' as fixed and comprehensible 'thing' to dissolve" (44). The belief in conjure and its power is based on an African worldview that differs from the Western view. If Western philosophy seeks to "comprehend and control fluidity," Baker wrote, "African conjure mean[s] to move the spirit through a fluid repertoire of 'forms'" (47). Spirit, then, in this philosophy, cannot be contained in, or defined by, any particular form.

It is not difficult to understand the appeal of such a philosophy to a people who, under slavery, were considered to be "chattel," mere things, like a mule or a load of lumber. Through the power of conjure, as seen in Baker's examination of Charles W. Chesnutt's late nineteenth-century collection of stories *The Conjure Woman*, the spirit could be set free of imprisoning form, as "black men . . . are transformed through conjure into seasonal vegetation figures, or trees, or gray wolves. . . . A black child is changed into a hummingbird and a mockingbird. A black woman becomes a cat" (Baker, 44). If conjure could be used to set the spirit free, to disguise and to protect, it could also be used to imprison the spirit. In one of Chesnutt's stories an abusive slaveholder is transformed through the power of conjure into a newly purchased slave and then turned over to the slaveholder's own cruel overseer.[3]

Kincaid's early work reflects a world in which conjure is a central force. References to conjure in *At the Bottom of the River* are numerous. They include the woman who removes her skin and then goes to "drink the blood of her secret enemies" (6), and the long-dead man who stands under a tree in his nice white suit. The lights in the mountains are likely to be the eyes of a "jablesse," a person "who can turn into anything" (9), and a stillborn child may be the result of "someone . . . sprinkling a colorless powder outside a closed door" (11). In this world, as the mother in the story "Girl" warns, one must never assume that things are what they appear to be. Constant alertness is required, because every action must take into account not only the visible world but also an equally real magical dimension: "Don't pick people's flowers—you might catch something; don't throw stones at blackbirds, because it might not be a blackbird at all" (5).

In this world, neither things nor people can be trusted to be what they seem. In *At the Bottom of the River* the person least to be trusted is the mother, who is capable of remarkable and usually sinister acts of self-transformation. In the story "My Mother" she turns herself into a serpent and then transforms her daughter as well, the two traveling along on their "white underbell[ies,]" their "tongue[s] darting and flickering in the hot air" (55). Other transformations are implied, imagined, or dreamed. In a dream, the beautiful mother who "can change everything" tells her child about the jablesse. Then she adds, with the sinister mockery that the mother figure in Kincaid's work frequently displays, "Take good care when you see a beautiful woman. A jablesse always tries to look like a beautiful woman" (9). In the early stories it is the mother who has the power to transform herself; the daughter is the victim of this power. In the story "At Last" the daughter struggles to grasp a dangerously shifting reality: "What are you now? A young woman. But what are you really?" (13).

As *At the Bottom of the River* progresses, we begin to see the daughter coming into her own power of self-transformation, becoming a practitioner rather than a victim. In "My Mother" and in the collection's final, title story, Kincaid seems to be taking us inside the very process of transformation, showing how it feels to undergo a metamorphosis from one thing to another and the new sense of fearlessness that accompanies this ability.

For the daughter in "My Mother," this transformative power seems to correspond to the changes taking place as she moves from childhood to maturity: "I was no longer a child but I was not yet a woman. My skin had just blackened and cracked and fallen away and my new impregnable carapace had taken full hold. My nose had flattened; my hair curled in and stood out straight from my head simultaneously; my many rows of teeth in their retractable trays were in place" (56). Here the power of transformation is new and awkward, and it is not entirely clear how it will be used or to what advantage: "I let out a horrible roar, then a self-pitying whine. I had grown big, but my mother was bigger, and that would always be so" (56).

In the final story, however, "At the Bottom of the River," the transformed narrator is now able to see into a new world. Here a young woman who is exploring life's "terrain," a woman recovering from the breakdown seen in the story "Blackness," looks down to the bottom of the river where she sees a woman "the color of brown clay, [who] looked like a statue, liquid and gleaming, just before it is to be put in a kiln" (77). This woman directs the narrator's gaze to a new world, one in which "many things [are] blessed with unquestionable truth and purpose and beauty" (78). We see that the narrator has become the woman at the bottom of the river, and she is also, still, the woman standing on the bank of the river looking down: "I . . . looked back up at myself as I stood on the bank of the mouth of the river" (78). The seeking woman standing above, the self now seen, takes on titanic proportions, and her skin is "the red of flames when a fire burns alone in a darkened place" (79). The speaker is now "not myself as I had once known myself to be" (79), and in a process suggestive of the curative obeah bath that will later appear in *Annie John*, she feels as if she has been "dipped again and again, over and over, in a large vat filled with some precious elements"

(80). Rather than being one thing, she now feels herself to be multidimensional, like a "prism, many-sided and transparent, refracting and reflecting light as it reached me, light that never could be destroyed. And how beautiful I became" (80).

In coming into her own transformational power, the protagonist experiences at last the secret of this power. The transformation of things from one form to another is only significant in that it signals the insignificance of form. Power comes from feeling oneself to be beyond form and thus beyond the control of others, incapable of being classified, explained, or "named." Only then, paradoxically, does one have a name, a name that is not a label attached by others but wells up out of one's sense of self. Thus, at the end of "At the Bottom of the River," the protagonist says, "I . . . now feel myself grow solid and complete, my name filling up my mouth" (82).

Without the ability to see oneself in multiple dimensions, Kincaid's work says, there can be no true identity. Certainly this is a universal theme and one frequently seen in the coming-of-age process. But it also seems true that this is a theme particularly crucial to people whose lives, identities, and names have been seen as the possession of others, as is the case of people of African descent in the Americas. In later writing, Kincaid spells out the difference between the self-naming that wells up out of a sense of one's own liberated self and the labeling that is done to one by others and amounts to a kind of murder: "This naming of things is so crucial to possession—a spiritual padlock with the key thrown irretrievably away—that it is a murder, an erasing, and it is not surprising that when people have felt themselves prey to it (conquest), among their first acts of liberation is to change their names (Rhodesia to Zimbabwe, LeRoi Jones to Amiri Baraka)" ("Flowers," 159). And it was, of course, one of Elaine Potter Richardson's first acts of liberation to change her name to Jamaica Kincaid.

Though obeah powers and practice are treated as a simple fact of life in *Annie John*, neither mother nor daughter undergoes the magical transformations they do in *At the Bottom of the River*. Still, we recognize changes in *Annie John*, changes corresponding to those seen in *At the Bottom of the River*. The mother is not literally transformed from woman to serpent, but she is changed from the source of all love and delight to the embodiment of treachery and the symbol of death. The mother's once-beloved hand is now seen as "white and bony, as if it had long been dead and had been left out in the elements" (*AJ*, 30). Correspondingly, the girl does not literally shed her skin to grow a new hard carapace, but we see a progress that is similar to that of the girl in *At the Bottom of the River*. At the beginning, Annie is like the daughter in "Girl," virtually mesmerized by her mother's powerful voice, nearly mute to defend herself against her mother's sudden verbal assaults. But, by the end of *Annie John*, we see, as in *At the Bottom of the River*, a girl who is no longer paralyzed, who has emerged from the soft black cloud of soot that fills the air in both books (*BR*, 46; *AJ*, 112) to step into her own new life and to assume her own name. The girl in *Annie John* is always called "Little Miss" by her parents, but the first words in her mind as she wakes on the morning of her departure from Antigua are "My name is Annie John."

While mother and daughter in *Annie John* do not enter the magical dimension as completely and literally as do their counterparts in *At the Bottom of the River*, their lives are dominated by the knowledge that they could at any time be the victims of an obeah spell cast upon them by the former lovers of Annie's father. To guard against this, Annie and her mother must sometimes sit together in an obeah bath,

> in which the barks and flowers of many different trees, together with all sorts of oils, were boiled in the same large caldron. We would then sit in this bath in a darkened room with a strange-smelling candle burning away. . . . We took these baths after my mother had consulted with her obeah woman, and with her mother and a trusted friend, and all three of them had confirmed that from the look of things around our house . . . one of the many women my father had loved, had never married, but with whom he had had children was trying to harm my mother and me by setting bad spirits on us. (*AJ*, 14–15)

Indeed, an obeah spell is suspected when Annie suddenly suffers a physical and emotional breakdown, and a local obeah woman, Ma Jolie, is called in to administer a number of obeah remedies:

> She made cross marks on the soles of my feet, on my knees, on my stomach, in my armpits, and on my forehead. She lit two special candles and placed one over the head of my bed and the other near the foot. . . . She burned some incense in one corner of my room. She put a dozen tiny red candles—with white paper on their bottoms, to keep them afloat—in a basin of thick yellow oil. . . . In the basin with the candles she had placed scraps of paper on which were written the names of people who had wanted to harm me, most of them women my father had loved a long time ago. (*AJ*, 116–17)

Annie's sickness, however, is too much for Ma Jolie; this is a job for Ma Chess, Annie's grandmother and an obeah woman who knows "at least ten times more" than Ma Jolie. If the special bath is the baptism of obeah, Ma Chess constantly reconsecrates herself, bathing "once a month or so, in water in which things animal and vegetable had been boiled for a long time. Before she took this bath, she first swam in the sea" (*AJ*, 124). We see her, like the young woman at the end of *At the Bottom of the River*, dipped "again and again, over and over, in a large vat filled with some precious elements" (*BR*, 80).

With Ma Chess, Kincaid shows us real power, power that goes beyond the standard formulas of Ma Jolie. Not only does Ma Chess have the ability to discover what has actually possessed the girl, but she is also able to counteract this evil with an energy that seems to well up from a self that is perfectly integrated with the power of nature. Ma Chess sees instantly that Annie's illness is not the result of the type of spell that has been suspected; Annie is suffering a deeper and much more complex crisis of loss. Ma Chess's cure is not to give the child an obeah bath but to return her metaphorically to the first, amniotic bath, as she symbolically regestates Annie: "I would lie on my side, curled up like a little comma, and Ma Chess would lie next to me, curled up like a bigger comma, into which I fit" (*AJ*, 126).

By the end of *Annie John*, we come to understand that the magical, transformative, and curative powers attributed to the obeah woman only serve as a metaphor for the power of a woman who knows herself to be a part of the natural world and the vessel of its fertility, who keeps that connection by continually immersing herself in the natural element, and who is able to use her power to bathe and restore one whose own connection has been broken.

Jamaica Kincaid writes about the practice of obeah or conjure in a world where magical transformation is a commonly perceived reality. Kincaid also uses conjure magic as a metaphor for life's transformations, particularly the transformation from childhood to womanhood. But Kincaid's work can also be seen as itself a form of conjure. If conjure transformations can be used to cure and to curse, they can also be used to mask and to disguise, and Kincaid's work can be read on some level as an act of conjure, as a complex effort to mask and manipulate in which "sensible communication" with readers—readers whom Kincaid, publishing in the *New Yorker*, assumes to be "white people in the suburbs" (Cudjoe, 401)—is intentionally obscured. Consciously or unconsciously, Kincaid manipulates form in order to disguise and protect herself as she tests the extent to which her white readership is willing and able to respond to the work of a person of African descent whose life has been powerfully and painfully shaped by white domination. It is a domination that, as Kincaid's later work makes clear, is ongoing, even though slavery and colonialism have formally ended, and from whose effects—not the least of which is an abiding anger—she feels she will never be free.

These themes explode out of Kincaid's later work, and many reviewers of *A Small Place* found Kincaid's anger at colonial and racial oppression all too visible. The writing was viewed as "distorted" by a rage "which backs the reader into a corner," (Hill, 19) and seen as "shrill [and] radically subjective [so that it] serves only to alienate."[4]

The two works that put Kincaid on the literary map, *At the Bottom of the River* and *Annie John*, back no one into a corner, and the theme of oppression is nearly undetectable. *At the Bottom of the River* was read by reviewers as either beautiful and obscure or deeply personal, and *Annie John* was read as a dark but typical coming-of-age story that is so "familiar it could be happening in Anchorage, so inevitable it could be happening to any of us, anywhere, any time, any place."[5] Themes of racism and colonialism are not mentioned in most commentaries on these works; rather, readers tend to universalize the story instead of reading it in a political context. Even those critics who are attuned to "the politics of colonialism" acknowledge the largely "personal" nature of Kincaid's first two works. Donna Perry observed that "Jamaica Kincaid is not a 'political' writer in the sense that the Jamaican writer Michelle Cliff is," although Perry also found that Kincaid's "references to oppression suggest that in later works she might more fully explore the political implications of colonialism."[6]

Why are these themes, so prevalent in the later work, all but invisible in *At the Bottom of the River* and *Annie John*? It is interesting to compare Kincaid to Charles W. Chesnutt, whose collection *The Conjure Woman* features Uncle Julius, who tells conjure tales in the colorful dialect "an ignorant old southern Negro would be supposed to speak" (Chesnutt quoted in Baker, 42). As Baker showed, Chesnutt not only tells stories about conjure but also uses writing as a method of conjure. The stories are told by Uncle Julius to a fictitious northern white couple, as they are told by Chesnutt to his assumed white readers. Although the stories are offered as entertainment, Baker demonstrated that hidden in the magical "nonsense" stories and the amusing "dialect" language (e.g., "Well, I dunno wh'r you b'lieves in cunj'in'er not,—some er de w'ite folks don't, er says dey don't,—but de truf er de mattr is dat dis yer ole vimya'd is goophered" [Chesnutt, 11]) are accounts of the anguish of slavery, the separation of families, and the callousness, at best, of the white slave-holders. These stories of misery are disguised as light entertainment, since both Chesnutt and his narrator, talking to whites who have come south after the Civil War, know that they will meet too much resistance to have an effect if they tell the story of slavery's horrors directly. Their white listeners are not prepared to be backed into a corner by black rage at white oppression or by a direct challenge to the white world's view of itself. Instead, Chesnutt hides the real story behind the mask of the entertainer, the spinner of "nonsense" tales, as his hearers frequently term them. Baker wrote,

> The old man [the narrator, Uncle Julius] knows the sounds [folk stories, dialect] that are dear to the hearts of his white boss and his wife, and he presents them with conjuring efficaciousness. In effect, he presents a world in which "dialect" masks the drama of African spirituality chal-lenging and changing the disastrous transformations of slavery. . . . The *sound* of African ancestry operates at a low, signifying, and effective regis-ter *behind* the mask of a narrational dialect. . . . Finally what is sharply modified by the transformative soundings of the work are the dynamics of lordship and bondage as a whole. . . . One might say that Julius has secured . . . an enclave in which a venerable Afro-American spirit can sound off. During all of the black narrator's tellings, the white Ohioan believes the stories are merely expressive of a minstrel type. He views Julius as, at best, a useful entertainment, one who can do odd jobs *and* tell stories. He considers him, at worst, an agent of annoyance and crafti-ness—never as a potent force of African transformations that can not be comprehended or controlled by Western philosophy. (44–45)

Both Chesnutt and Uncle Julius, then, are protected by the mask of the entertainer. At the same time, enough of the true story of slavery is revealed, the real story that Chesnutt wants to tell, so that it can be detected by those (such as the white boss's invalid wife, Anne) who are willing to hear it. Anne's sympathy allows her to "sweep past" the incredible nature of the conjure stories, wrote Robert M. Farnsworth in a 1969 introduction to Chesnutt's book, to arrive at "the response Chesnutt hoped his larger reading audience would share—'What a sys-tem [slavery] was'" (xiii).

Kincaid, too, seems to be using form to disguise and protect herself as she, like Chesnutt, tests the reaction of her white readership. The responses the boss and his more sensitive wife give to Uncle Julius's stories, and the responses of reviewers to Kincaid's *At the Bottom of the River* are strikingly similar. The white boss, John, sees Julius's stories as nonsense, entertaining primarily for their colorful dialect and for their improbable fantasy. Likewise, reviewers praised Kincaid's first work for its "care for language and joy in the sheer sounds of words" (Tyler, 33), but found them, if not exactly nonsensical, then "too personal and too peculiar to translate into any sort of sensible communication" (Milton, 22). Another reviewer found something childlike in the work: "What Kincaid has to tell us, she tells, with her singsong style, in a series of images that are as sweet and mysterious as the secrets that children whisper in your ear." The "risk," this reviewer wrote, is that "not everyone is willing to decipher the secrets."[7] One reviewer sees the obscurity of *At the Bottom of the River* as a trick to impress the reader, as the writer "spin[s] lovely, airy webs with a sidelong glance in our direction every now and then to see if we're appreciative" (Tyler, 33). Similarly, John wonders whether Uncle Julius's stories camouflage some petty scheme for his own advancement.

To some extent, Kincaid's early work is a trick. The stories do mesmerize with their rich, rhythmic language, and they are difficult to read as conventional, linear accounts. Still, the sense is there for those willing to work for it, and Kincaid seems to be operating on the assumption that those who are truly receptive will be able, as was Uncle Julius's more sympathetic female listener, to "sweep past" these distractions and to hear the underlying sound.

For some of these readers, the mother-daughter theme is "the major preoccupation of Kincaid's work."[8] Like Chesnutt's sensitive Anne, many of Kincaid's readers also detect the "universal" story of loss that is disguised by the mask of language and nonsense. As Anne could imagine the grief of disrupted families, even if they were slave families, so many of Kincaid's readers can imagine the grief of lost childhood, and a lost sense of the world's loving perfection, even if this loss is experienced by people different from themselves.

But, as Farnsworth showed, even the sensitive Anne was "too civilized" to delve more deeply into Chesnutt's story and so failed "to realize the intimacy of the black's identification with the mysterious natural forces" and to grasp "the power of the black world, the mysterious natural world that challenges [the] common assumptions of the supremacy of the white man's world" (xiv, xvi). Similarly, few if any of Kincaid's reviewers in the popular press find the assumptions of the white, Western world challenged in the early work. Only a handful of critics, such as Giovanna Covi, have detected this theme. In a reading influenced by Jacques Derrida and others, Covi saw in Kincaid a distinct metaphysical challenge to the Western worldview. Both *At the Bottom of the River* and *Annie John*, she explained, "break though the objective, metaphysical linearity" of Western tradition in a way that is "not only disruptive of the institutional order, but also revolutionary in its continuous self-criticism and its rejection of all labels" (345). Kincaid's work disrupts "binary oppositions," creating a world in which "everything is ambiguous, multiple, fragmented. Blackness is the night that 'falls in silence' as well as the racial color that 'flows through [her] veins' [*BR*, 46], but above all it is what cannot be defined—a signifier that escapes its signified by a continuous shifting. . . . It is identity together with the annihilation of the self" (Covi, 347). Covi likened this sense of ambiguity, multiplicity and fragmentation to "the broken rhythm of jazz . . . a cry of protest against the symmetry of the racist division of society" (346).

If Kincaid's writing works to disrupt "binary oppositions" upon which the Western worldview and Western society are based, it also begins, as Baker said of Chesnutt, to "sound" a story of "Afro-American transformative resourcefulness" under the guise of "speaking *nonsense*" (46). But Kincaid's challenge to the Western worldview, even in the first two works, is not entirely disguised, for, with Kincaid's later work as a guide, we are able to see her in *At the Bottom of the River* beginning to undertake a work of transformation not only upon the European worldview but also upon the European conqueror. Even in this early work, Kincaid was beginning to focus on this conqueror, in whose brilliance and superiority Kincaid and other Caribbean children have been taught to believe.

This conqueror makes his first appearance in the final, title story of *At the Bottom of the River*. He is in no way named or identified here. But his characteristics are similar to those of another figure, Ovando, the empty European conqueror found in Kincaid's 1989 story of the same name.[9] With Ovando in mind, we may understand that it is a similar figure who blots the landscape and impedes the protagonist's journey through the "terrain" of existence in "At the Bottom of the River." The "change" that is being worked here is the transformation of the European conqueror from the grand, beneficent, entirely beautiful figure of colonial myth into an empty man, entirely cut off from nature, unable to "conceive of the union of opposites, or, for that matter their very existence" (*BR*, 63).

As Chesnutt's conjure tale transforms the master into a "noo nigger," a newcomer slave upon which the master's own cruel overseer inflicts abuse, so Kincaid's story strips the white colonial "master" of overtly identifying characteristics before it inflicts on him the stereotyping, dehumanizing, negative definition that has traditionally marked the white world's definition of the black person. If Kincaid has been "erased" by colonialism, she now, subtly, begins the erasure of the colonizer. She describes him only by what he is not:

> He cannot conceive of how emotions varying in color and intensity, will rapidly heighten, reach an unbearable pitch, then finally explode in the silence of the evening air. He cannot conceive of the chance invention that changes again and again and forever the great turbulence that is human history. Not for him can thought crash over thought in random and violent succession, leaving his brain suffused in contradiction. He sits in nothing, this man: not in a full space, not in emptiness, not in darkness, not in light or glimmer of. He sits in nothing, in nothing, in nothing. (BR, 64)

Like Chesnutt, and like Chesnutt's narrator, Uncle Julius, Kincaid works her changes on the white conqueror subtly. Not only do white readers not feel challenged or threatened, but they are barely aware that what they are reading is the beginning of their own definition.

With success, however, Chesnutt's "racial statement became more blunt and challenging. . . . He wanted very much to believe that America was inviting him to tell the story of the Afro-American from his point of view" (Farnsworth, in Chesnutt, xviii). In the same way, with success Kincaid's statement became more blunt and challenging. Her third book-length work, A Small Place, begins with a portrait of tourists on Antigua and contains the lines "You are a tourist . . . to be frank, white" (4) and "A tourist is an ugly human being" (14). Kincaid, like Chesnutt, seems to have dropped the mask of harmless entertainer, not because she felt more rage over white domination than before but, as Farnsworth said of Chesnutt, because she had come to feel an acceptance that seemed to invite her to tell the real story. In speaking of A Small Place, which was rejected by the New Yorker, the magazine that had published all of her other work, Kincaid says, "It had a sort of traumatic history because it was so intimate. It was written for the readers of the New Yorker, whom I had come to think of as friends in some peculiar way" (Perry interview, 132).

At this point, however, the similarity between Chesnutt and Kincaid comes to an end. Chesnutt's book *The Marrow of Tradition* received a "cool public reception," according to Farnsworth. The author "decided the time was not yet" and gave up writing for a successful law career (xix). But while *A Small Place* was initially rejected for publication, it went on to find a prestigious publisher, Farrar, Straus and Giroux. And although some British reviewers despised the book, finding it "shrill" (Fonseca) and "sniveling" (Maja-Pearce), and warned Kincaid that the British, at least, are not "about to discover the dubious delights of self-flagellation" (Maja-Pearce), American reviewers received it more calmly. Michiko Kakutani, in the *New York Times*, observed that Kincaid's "observations concerning contemporary, self-ruled Antigua . . . tend to be just as unsparing as her assessments of its colonial condition." Hilton Als described Kincaid's voice in *A Small Place* as "disagreeable and stunning as it need be," as she "name[s] the world" in a "language that is completely hers."[10] And Peggy Ellsberg noted that the book ends with an appeal to the common humanity of all, a mutual understanding that is possible only after power relationships are given up.[11]

While *A Small Place* has failed to gain acceptance in some quarters, it has not ended Kincaid's career and she has not ceased to write in the same tone. The novel *Lucy*, which followed *A Small Place* by two years, has been received favorably by most American reviewers, even though it fixes a direct and unflattering gaze on the sophisticated and well-to-do Americans among whom Kincaid's protagonist now finds herself. Lucy's employer, the loving and well-intentioned Mariah, is shown to be blind to the implications of her own position of privilege. She simply does not grasp, for example, the relationship between her luxurious life-style and the environmental destruction she abhors. Mariah's husband, Lewis, is coolly calculating, "used to getting his way," and able to cause others to "blunder into defeat" (119). Though Mariah is loving and Lewis is cold, both assume the privileges of race and class and share a blindness to the way in which these are bought at the expense of others.

If *A Small Place* did not end Kincaid's career, neither did it use up her anger. Following the publication of *Lucy*, Kincaid turned once again to the essay form. Her "On Seeing England for the First Time" describes the "erasure" of black children by a colonial educational system that depicted a world revolving around England, and her furious reaction on first seeing the reality of a land and a culture that had been presented to her in fairy-tale terms. She found not a brilliant and superior race, cul-

46 JAMAICA KINCAID

ture and climate, but "weather . . . like a jail sentence; the English are a
very ugly people; the food in England is like a jail sentence; the hair of
English people is so straight, so dead-looking; the English have an
unbearable smell so different from the smell of people I know, real people of course" ("SE," 16). Her reaction is one of rage, for it is the fairy
tale of England, the dream of a brilliant England conjured up by colonial
authorities, that has robbed her of herself.

Unlike Chesnutt, Kincaid has been able to emerge from behind the
mask of harmless entertainer to speak directly about the ongoing pain of
domination of one group by another, the continued assumption of superiority and the murderous anger this can engender. She no longer "hyp-
notizes" her readers with beautiful but obscure prose. Her shifting of the
balance of power by portraying those who live for power as empty and
dead, her erasure in these works of those who would erase others, is no
longer carried on in secret. But in emerging from the magical obscurity
of *At the Bottom of the River* to the enraged directness of *A Small Place* and
"On Seeing England for the First Time"—in writing, in Toni Morrison's
words, "the truth about the interior life"[12]—Kincaid has surely per-
formed the most important conjure act of all, the "transformation of the
black-as-object into the black-as-subject."[13]

Chapter Four

Rhythm and Repetition: Kincaid's Incantatory Lists

One of the most striking aspects of Jamaica Kincaid's style is its use of rhythmic repetition to produce a sound that is variously described as incantatory, magical, or religious. As with most magical and religious incantations, the spell is cast for a reason. A Kincaid sentence, Derek Walcott said, "heads toward its own contradiction" in works that are "full of spiritual contradictions clarified" (quoted in Garis, 80). Kincaid's rhythms and repetitions, the long, seemingly artless, listlike sentences charm and lull the reader, disguising what is actually happening, which is that one thing is being transformed into another. The mesmerizing repetitions have the effect of putting the reader into the world of Kincaid's psyche, a world in which one reality constantly slides into another under cover of the ordinary rhythms of life.

The rhythm and repetition of Kincaid's prose signal a clash of contradictions. At the same time, they work to manipulate a reader into accepting the contradictions that are being offered. In the story "Girl," for example, the mother's chant of information and advice enfolds and ensnares the daughter, rendering her nearly helpless before the mother's transforming will. In *Annie John*, rhythm, repetition, and list signal contradiction and manipulation, but increasingly these devices also mark a response to impending loss. The mother's beloved homemaking energy, including her celebration of her child, is cataloged at the very moment that energy is being turned against the child, destroying her sense of home. In Kincaid's later work, however, such as the long essay *A Small Place*, it is the assumed white reader who is immobilized by the rhythms of the prose, as Kincaid's protagonist graduates from being the victim of such transformative power to a practitioner in her own right.

Kincaid's "Girl," the first story in *At the Bottom of the River*, may be read as a kind of primer in the manipulative art of rhythm and repetition. The story begins with the mother's voice giving such simple, benevolent, and appropriately maternal advice as "Wash the white clothes on Monday and put them on the stone heap; wash the color

clothes on Tuesday and put them on the clothesline to dry; . . ." (*BR*, 3).
Like the girl to whom the mother speaks, the reader is lulled and drawn
in by the chant of motherly admonitions, which go on to advise about
how to dress for the hot sun, how to cook pumpkin fritters, how to buy
cloth for a blouse, and how to prepare fish. Seduced in only a few lines,
readers, like the listening girl, are caught unawares by an admonition
that sounds like the previous, benevolent advice but has in fact suddenly
veered in a new direction, uniting the contradictions of nurture and
condemnation: ". . . always eat your food in such a way that it won't
turn someone else's stomach; on Sundays try to walk like a lady and not
like the slut you are so bent on becoming. . ." (*BR*, 3).

As the brief, one-sentence story progresses, we come to see that the
mother's speech, inviting with nurturing advice, on the one hand, and
repelling with condemnatory characterization, on the other, not only
manipulates the girl into receptivity to the mother's condemning view
but also teaches the art of manipulation. The mother incorporates into
her indictment of the girl's impending sluttishness the task of teaching
her how to hide that condition: ". . . this is how to hem a dress when you
see the hem coming down and so to prevent yourself from looking like
the slut I know you are so bent on becoming" (*BR*, 4). As the contradictions draw closer together—as nurture and manipulation become
increasingly intertwined—the language seems to become even more
rhythmic:

> . . . this is how you smile to someone you don't like too much; this is how
> you smile to someone you don't like at all; this is how you smile to some-
> one you like completely; this is how you set a table for tea; this is how
> you set a table for dinner; this is how you set a table for dinner with an
> important guest; this is how you set a table for lunch; this is how you set
> a table for breakfast; this is how you behave in the presence of men who
> don't know you very well, and this way they won't recognize immediate-
> ly the slut I have warned you against becoming. . . (*BR*, 4)

In the last third of "Girl," the mother's voice continues the litany of
domestic instruction, but added now is comment on a frighteningly contradictory world, one in which nothing is ever what it seems to be. The
continued tone of motherly advice at first works to lighten the sinister
nature of the information imparted and then, paradoxically, to make
these disclosures even more frightening; eventually we see that in a
world in which a recipe for stew slides into a recipe for the death of a
child, nothing is safe:

. . . don't pick people's flowers—you might catch something; don't throw stones at blackbirds, because it might not be a blackbird at all; this is how to make bread pudding; this is how to make doukona; this is how to make pepper pot; this is how to make a good medicine for a cold; this is how to make a good medicine to throw away a child before it even becomes a child; this is how to catch a fish; this is how to throw back a fish you don't like, and that way something bad won't fall on you. (*BR*, 5)

In the collection's second story, "In the Night," a comfortable domestic world is again casually transformed into the site of a life-and-death struggle and then casually changed back. The repetitive language first comforts with its invocation of familiar and simple activities but then horrifies as it veers into the suggestion that there is little difference between making a dress and killing a child: ". . . someone is making a basket, someone is making a girl a dress or a boy a shirt, someone is making her husband a soup with cassava so that he can take it to the cane field tomorrow, someone is making his wife a beautiful mahogany chest, someone is sprinkling a colorless powder outside a closed door so that someone else's child will be stillborn. . ." (*BR*, 11).

The story "In the Night" ends with a fantasy in which the girl imagines that she will one day marry a woman whom we take to be her mother, "a red-skin woman with black bramblebush hair and brown eyes, who wears skirts that are so big I can easily bury my head in them" and who, each night will tell a story that begins, 'Before you were born.'" (*BR*, 11–12). The two will live in a "mud hut near the sea," and the fantasy proceeds as a list of domestic furnishings and tools, one of the numerous such lists found in Kincaid's work.

With this story we encounter something new. Now it is the girl, not the mother, who slides one reality into another under cover of life's ordinary rhythms. Contained in the following list are both a vision of mother and daughter living together eternally in simple domestic bliss and a literal portrait of the inevitable collapse of this union:

In the mud hut will be two chairs and one table, a lamp that burns kerosene, a medicine chest, a pot, one bed, two pillows, two sheets, one looking glass, two cups, two saucers, two dinner plates, two forks, two drinking-water glasses, one china pot, two fishing strings, two straw hats to ward the hot sun off our heads, two trunks for things we have very little use for, one basket, one book of plain paper, one box filled with twelve

crayons of different colors, one loaf of bread wrapped in a piece of brown
paper, one coal pot, one picture of two women standing on a jetty, one
picture of the same two women embracing, one picture of the same two
women waving goodbye, one box of matches. (*BR*, 11–12)

Here the "pictures" of the two women are ambiguous, certainly intentionally so. The two women could have come to the jetty to wave goodbye to a third person, or they could be waving goodbye to one another.
And we do not know who they are; they could be mother and daughter
or someone else. Readers of *Annie John*, however, will see here a fore-
shadowing of that book's final chapter, "A Walk to the Jetty," in which
Annie and her mother embrace, wave goodbye, and then part, as Annie
leaves Antigua, seemingly forever. Thus, the fantasy of eternal mother-
daughter union is transformed into separation, even as it is being constructed. From this vantage point, even the picture of the embrace
cannot be seen as the unambiguous demonstration of affection it seems
to be, for if this is a preview of the final scene of *Annie John*, the embrace
is, rather than a demonstration of affectionate union, one last struggle
for power as the mother holds the girl so tightly that she cannot breathe
and the girl, "suddenly on [her] guard," asks herself, "What does she
want now?" (*AJ*, 147).

    In the last, title story of *At the Bottom of the River*, we see Kincaid
changing the nature and purpose of the incantatory list. As the mother
uses it to both invite and denounce, the daughter uses it as a way of both
holding on and breaking free. Again and again, we will see this effect in
Kincaid's work as her protagonists, as if to gain some control over life's
eternal changeability, list the contents of a world from which they must
soon depart. As the mother in Kincaid's work uses her repetitious chants
to control others, the daughter uses them to control herself, appearing to
steady herself by chanting out the properties of a beloved world even as
she prepares to leave it. We remember that Kincaid and her characters—
mothers and daughters—are women caught between worlds, and perhaps it is only in this way that the duality can be managed.

    This connection between the listing of beloved objects and departure
becomes clear at the end of this final story, as the protagonist emerges
from the "pit" of an existential crisis in which she confronts her own
inevitable death. The acceptance of the inevitability of this final and ulti-
mate departure is signaled by a listing of domestic items that seems to
symbolize all the beauty, simplicity, and perishability of human life. It is
as if in reciting the list of homely items, the story's protagonist joins with

them as a part of all life, rather than feeling herself alone and apart in her fate:

> Emerging from my pit . . . I step into a room and I see that the lamp is lit. In the light of the lamp, I see some books, I see a chair, I see a table, I see a pen; I see a bowl of ripe fruit, a bottle of milk, a flute made of wood, the clothes that I will wear. And as I see these things in the light of the lamp, all perishable and transient, how bound up I know I am to all that is human endeavor, to all that is past and to all that shall be, to all that shall be lost and leave no trace. (*BR*, 81–82)

If an increase in rhythmic, repetitious language seems to mark a crescendo of contradictions in *At the Bottom of the River*, the extensive listings of domestic items may be used to chart an intensified sense of loss, or imminent loss, in *Annie John*. In the book's second chapter, "The Circling Hand," in which Annie's mother first harshly announces a change in their formerly close relationship, listings of domestic items abound. Most of the lists catalog the mother's activities, her shopping, her cooking ("pumpkin soup with droppers, banana fritters with salt fish stewed in antroba and tomatoes, fungie with salt fish stewed in antroba and tomatoes. . ." [17]), or her laundry methods. Most striking is the page-long list of Annie's baby and childhood paraphernalia which fill the mother's trunk, from her first garment, a white chemise sewed by the mother, to her first jewelry, her report cards and certificates of merit from Sunday school. Annie will, of course, be banished from all such sites of maternal activity within a few pages, apparently as a result of her impending maturity. No longer will she be allowed to be her mother's little shadow, and sorting through the beloved trunk is one of the first shared pleasures to go, as the mother declares that they no longer have time for such things.

In the last chapter of *Annie John*, "A Walk to the Jetty," Annie prepares to leave Antigua, and once again list making flourishes as Annie, on the morning of her departure, catalogs the morning sounds in her house, the contents of her room, the breakfast menu, and finally the significant events of her childhood as they are suggested by the various sites she must pass on her walk to the jetty. These things and places are not only dear and familiar; they are Annie's very life, and there is a kind of death in leaving them. Now the domestic lists take on an increasingly rhythmic form, as Annie seeks to set the moment of departure to the ongoing beat of daily life:

The house we live in my father built with his own hands. The bed I am lying in my father built with his own hands. If I get up and sit on a chair, it is a chair my father built with his own hands. When my mother uses a large wooden spoon to stir the porridge we sometimes eat as part of our breakfast, it will be a spoon that my father has carved with his own hands. . . . The nightie I am wearing, with scalloped neck and hem and sleeves, my mother made with her own hands. When I look at things in a certain way, I suppose I should say that the two of them made me with their own hands. . . . Lying in my bed for the last time, I thought, This is what I add up to. (*AJ*, 132–33)

Kincaid's protagonist insists that she is glad to leave it all, that she never again wants to hear the sheep being driven to pasture past her house or her mother dressing and gargling. As she lies in the half-dark looking at her room and all the things that "had meant a lot" to her, she declares, "My heart could have burst open with joy at the thought of never having to see any of it again" (*AJ*, 131–32). But this claim is contradicted by the energy expended on the lists and their great detail. Even her vow that her departure will be permanent is cast in terms of another, rhythmic, listing of the details of home: "I had made up my mind that, come what may, the road for me now went only in one direction: away from my home, away from my mother, away from my father, away from the everlasting blue sky, away from the everlasting hot sun, away from the people who said to me, 'This happened during the time your mother was carrying you'" (*AJ*, 133–34).

In *A Small Place* rhythm and repetition are once again used to manipulate an unsuspecting listener, this time Kincaid's assumed white reader, the "you" to whom the piece is addressed. Like the daughter in "Girl," the reader of *A Small Place* is not immediately put on guard against an assault, but rather drawn in by what seems to be a cheerful offer to discuss a pleasant subject. Here the subject is tourism in the Caribbean, and the essay's opening lines seem to set out a typical travel-writing invitation to dream of pleasurable experiences in exotic places, "If you go to Antigua as a tourist, this is what you will see" (*SP*, 3).

Like the mother's voice in "Girl," Kincaid's voice in *A Small Place* keeps up the reassuring litany of advice and information, even as it turns toward condemnation. True, there is, from the very beginning, a somewhat unusual and slightly unsettling focus on the vacationer—"You may be the sort of tourist who would . . ." (*SP*, 3)—but still it is possible to read on in relative comfort, to assume that this is the safe and satisfying piece of travel writing one is eager to enjoy.

Soon, however, as the phrase "you are a tourist" is repeated again and again, we come to see that is not merely a term of description. Rather, "you are a tourist" becomes an indictment, repeated as a sort of refrain after every fresh example of insensitive and dehumanizing behavior. At first, the phrase may seem to offer an excuse, to explain, for example, why the traveler is free to enjoy the hot, dry climate without ever wondering how constant drought may affect the island's inhabitants. But just as we have become nervous enough to form this comforting theory, it is exploded by the demonstration that the phrase "you are a tourist," rather than excusing the reader, is pulling him into a racially charged atmosphere, which he is intent on avoiding. The phrase is in fact a code for "you are white." Kincaid wrote, "You disembark from your plane. You go through customs. Since you are a tourist, a North American or European—to be frank, white—and not an Antiguan black returning to Antigua from Europe or North America with cardboard boxes of much needed cheap clothes and food for relatives, you move through customs swiftly, you move through customs with ease. Your bags are not searched" (*SP*, 4–5).

Soon it is clear that Kincaid is not writing about the tourist's destination as much as about the tourist, repeating "you are a tourist" and then "you are on holiday" as a drumbeat of indictment. The tourist is shown in many attitudes, but always he demonstrates a narcissistic determination to see Antigua and Antiguans in terms of his own desires and needs, never as a place and people with a separate existence. Even a dangerous road and bad drivers will be worked into the theme of holiday thrills in which the author's island home is transformed into one big amusement park: "Your driver is reckless; he is a dangerous man who drives in the middle of the road when he thinks no other cars are coming in the opposite direction, passes other cars on blind curves that run uphill, drives at sixty miles an hour on narrow, curving roads. . . . This might frighten you (you are on your holiday; you are a tourist); this might excite you (you are on holiday; you are a tourist)" (*SP*, 6).

In a few pages, then, Kincaid has reversed the usual situation. The reader who has, probably unconsciously, expected to dehumanize the natives with his narcissistic gaze, has been himself dehumanized, reduced to the stereotype "you are a tourist." Kincaid does not stop here. Again, she pulls the reader in by seeming to return to the expected travelogue. On viewing the sea, the tourist—always "you"—is transported: "Oh, what beauty! Oh, what beauty! You have never seen anything like this. You are so excited. You breathe shallow. You breathe deep." But swiftly, with the repetition of the phrase "you see yourself," even this seemingly innocuous moment is transformed into a portrait of the tourist whose determination to consume everything in sight renders him bloated and ugly. First, pleasantly enough, "you see a beautiful boy skimming the water, godlike, on a Windsurfer," and then, dangerously,

> you see an incredibly unattractive, fat, pastrylike-fleshed woman enjoying a walk on the beautiful sand, with a man, an incredibly unattractive, fat pastrylike-fleshed man; you see the pleasure they are taking in their surroundings. Still standing, looking out the window, you see yourself lying on the beach, enjoying the amazing sun. . . . You see yourself taking a walk on that beach, you see yourself meeting new people (only they are new in a very limited way, for they are people just like you). You see yourself eating some delicious, locally grown food. You see yourself, you see yourself. (SP, 13)

If you, the tourist, see yourself reduced to a dehumanized stereotype, Kincaid seems to say, perhaps you can see how you are connected to the people you had intended to dehumanize, to reduce to mere picturesque vacation scenery. At the end of this section, by repeating the phrase "every native," Kincaid joins white tourist and black Antiguan in common humanity:

> That the native does not like the tourist is not hard to explain. For every native of every place is a potential tourist, and every tourist is a native of somewhere. Every native everywhere lives a life of overwhelming and crushing banality and boredom and desperation and depression, and every deed, good and bad, is an attempt to forget this. Every native would like to find a way out, every native would like a rest, every native would like a tour. But some natives—most natives in the world—cannot go anywhere. They are too poor. They are too poor to go anywhere. They are too poor to escape the reality of their lives. (SP, 18–19)

In Kincaid's story "Ovando," a fantasy about a European conqueror of that name, the most striking rhythmic repetitions begin late in the story, as if the author, having set out Ovando's destructive deeds, only now cries out against them. Here, as elsewhere, an intensified sense of rhythm seems to mark an intensification of emotion. Now Ovando is no longer a man, but has become the "night," a deep, dark receptacle for all that is deadly and dreaded: "Ovando lived in the thickest part of the night, the deepest part of the night, the part of the night where all suffering dwells, including death; the part of the night in which the weight of the world is made visible and eternal terror is confirmed" (82). In the last lines of the story, as in the last section of *A Small Place*, Kincaid unites victim and victimizer in a shared fate. Here the repetition of "nothing" sounds a funereal chant for both those who dominate and those who are dominated. As is frequently the case, rhythm and repetition signal both loss and the struggle to survive it: "A charge against Ovando, then, is that he loved himself so that all other selves and all other things became nothing to him. I became nothing to Ovando. My relatives became nothing to Ovando. Everything that could trace its lineage through me became nothing to Ovando. And so it came to be that Ovando loved nothing, lived in nothing and died in just that way" (83).

In the novel *Lucy*, we can recognize Kincaid's voice and language, but the use of rhythm and repetition is much less pronounced. In the cool, gray world of an American city, the intensity that inspires the rhythmic passages in earlier works has been muted, and the voice is calmer and more analytical. This is a world without magic; magical transformations have been replaced by a rich family's disguises and pretenses, posturings that Lucy sees through effortlessly. It is not until late in the book, when Lucy begins to speak about the loss she felt when her mother's attention turned to a succession of baby brothers, that we get the first, long list, a litany of love and loss:

> As I was telling Mariah all these things, all sorts of little details of my life on the island where I grew up came back to me: the color of six o'clock in the evening sky on the day I went to call the midwife to assist my mother in the birth of my first brother; the white of the chemise that my mother embroidered for the birth of my second brother; the redness of the red ants that attacked my third brother as he lay in bed next to my mother a day after he was born; the navy blue of the sailor suit my first brother wore when my father took him to a cricket match; the absence of red lipstick on my mother's mouth after they were all born; the day the men from the prison in their black-and-white jail clothes came to cut down a plum tree that grew in our yard, because one of my brothers had almost choked to death swallowing whole a plum he picked up from the ground. (131)

The white chemise here is reminiscent of another garment, the white cotton gown that begins the list of beloved childhood items in Annie John's trunk. This echo allows us to see the world of change and loss contained in the passage above. The infant who replaces Annie in the

cherished white dress will himself be displaced, will be thrown out into a
world in which all things seem to be in physical and moral flux. The jux-
taposition of white chemise and biting red ants, of toddling children and
jail crews, and of ripe plums and the sudden threat of death whisks us
back to the dangerous magical world of Kincaid's earlier work, a world
in which the most innocent act may carry with it an unintentional pollu-
tion, as in "Girl": "Don't eat fruit on the street—flies will follow you"
(3–4). While this may not be the world Lucy lives in now, it is still the
world that lives in her.

   Lucy contains one other passage of rhythmic repetition, which, like
the lists at the end of *Annie John*, marks the protagonist's preparations to
leave one world for another:

> I used to be nineteen; I used to live in the household of Lewis and Mariah,
> and I used to be the girl who took care of their four children. . . . I used
> to see Mariah with happiness an essential part of her daily existence, and
> then, when the perfect world she had known for so long vanished without
> warning, I saw sadness replace it; I used to lie naked in moonlight with a
> boy named Hugh; I used to not know who Lewis was, until one day he
> revealed himself to be just another man, an ordinary man, when I saw
> him in love with his wife's best friend; I used to be that person, and I
> used to be in those situations. That was how I spent the year just past.
> (137–38)

Lucy has not yet told us she is leaving her employer to live on her own,
but the list signals impending change. Here again, we see a detailed
accounting of all that is soon to be left forever, as if this were a way of
continuing to have those things which are one's life, even as one prepares
to leave them forever.

Chapter Five

Kincaid and the Canon: In Dialogue with *Paradise Lost* and *Jane Eyre*

As a child schooled in the British colonial system, Jamaica Kincaid was nourished on a diet of English classics, reading from Shakespeare and Milton by the age of six. Sometimes the great works of English literature were administered as a punishment; for her schoolgirl crimes Kincaid was forced to memorize large chunks of *Paradise Lost*. Other works, such as Charlotte Brontë's *Jane Eyre*, were Kincaid's best friends, and she read them over and over.

In her relationship to the English language and the canonical works of English literature with which colonial children were so assiduously inculcated, Kincaid seems to present a paradox. The emphasis on England, Kincaid has said, the constant inference that England was the center of the universe, robbed colonial children of a sense of their own worth. Further, the rigorous study of English only enhanced the power of what Kincaid has called "the language of the criminal." This language, she believes, is inherently biased in favor of those who enslaved and continue to dominate her people: "For the language of the criminal can contain only the goodness of the criminal's deed. The language of the criminal can explain and express the deed only from the criminal's point of view. It cannot contain the horror of the deed, the injustice of the deed, the agony, the humiliation inflicted on me" (*SP*, 32).

But Kincaid sees another side to the colonial education. Works such as *Paradise Lost* taught her that the question of justice and injustice could be considered and articulated (Simmons). Though this was probably not the intention of the colonial educators, the young Kincaid found a hero she could identify with in *Paradise Lost*, the defiant and outcast Lucifer.

In her decision to use, rather than to repress, her colonial education, Kincaid may be in the vanguard of a new generation of post-colonial writers. In the past, according to Françoise Lionnet, herself a native of the small Indian Ocean nation of Mauritius, writers have tried to ignore colonial language and literary traditions in their efforts to find an authentic means of self-expression. But often they have been unable to find an alternative method of communication. More recently, Lionnet says, writers have "succeed[ed] in giving voice to their repressed traditions" through a "dialogue with the dominant discourses they hope to transform."[1] To refuse to use the dominant language and thereby to be silenced, she argues, is to continue to grant the power structure its own terms. Rather, Lionnet calls for a mixing, allowing those who were subjected to the rule of a culture very different from their own, one of whom she counts herself, to "nurture our differences without encouraging us to withdraw into new dead ends, without enclosing us within facile oppositional practises or sterile denunciations and disavowals. . . . On a textual level, we can choose authors across time and space and read them together for new insights" (Lionnet, 5–8). Kincaid, in her reinscription of the paradise-lost theme found in Milton, as well as in her rewriting of the story of a young woman's struggle for autonomy in Brontë's *Jane Eyre*, seems to do precisely this, to take these great works of English literature and to read them in her own terms, turning them to her own use.

Kincaid's relation to the paradise-lost theme, and Milton's work in particular, is complex. She both uses and subverts the European creation story to explore her own predicament. The story of the grief of Adam and Eve and of the rage of Lucifer at having been cast out of Paradise mirrors the anguish of each of Kincaid's young protagonists at having been cast out of her mother's love, which Annie sees as a lost "paradise" (*AJ*, 25). The theme of a lost paradise also parallels the story of the slaves and their descendants, people who have been cast out from the place where they were at home, where their existence seemed compatible with the beauty of creation, to a place where they would be eternally criminalized, though the crime can never be explained. They, like Lucifer, find themselves in a place of eternal loss, very much "unlike the place from whence they fell!"[2]

The paradise-lost story gives Kincaid a framework for exploring both forms of loss: Is her protagonist, a black girl coming of age in a colonial and racist society, guilty, like Lucifer, of some crime of pride against her betters? Has she, like Eve, been innocently tricked into some incomprehensible but unforgivable sin? Or are all three the victims of a narcissistic power whose idea of justice is informed entirely by the need to have its own perfection mirrored back to it?

Kincaid uses the paradise-lost story not only to study the predicament of those cast out but also to indict power, as exercised both by the mother and by colonial authority. Paradoxically, the creation story as told by Milton works well for this purpose. Milton saw his work as upholding the legitimacy of divine power, as justifying "the ways of God to men" (1.26). At the same time, *Paradise Lost* offers an unavoidably subversive reading of that divine power. With its humanly sympathetic Lucifer and insensitive God—at least in the early books—it tells a story of cold establishment rectitude and the criminalization of anyone who would do other than reflect establishment glory back to itself. Even if God is right and Lucifer is wrong in Milton's story, it is not too difficult to sympathize with Lucifer against a power-obsessed authority. And surely we cannot help admiring him for his stubborn refusal to "repent or change," though he fully understands the overwhelming power of his adversary (1.96).

Kincaid makes use of Milton's *Paradise Lost* throughout her work, studying the same problems that obsessed Milton: a power that does not justify itself (thus requiring others, like Milton, to do the job), a casting-out that cannot be explained. Milton's Satan is mirrored in Kincaid's protagonists who cannot help being dazzled by the brilliant power of authority—the magic and beauty of the mother, the "fairy tale" of England (*SP*, 42)—even as they feel themselves to be obliterated by that power, criminalized for attitudes other than the entirely worshipful, unable either to repent or change.

In *At the Bottom of the River*, Kincaid's protagonist, who, like Satan, finds herself in a "pit," emerges only by retelling the story of paradise. In Milton's work, the point of paradise and therefore the point of creation itself is power. This is true in God's heaven, where God and Lucifer war, and in the earthly garden from which Adam and Eve are expelled, more or less innocent bystanders, caught in the crossfire between God and Satan. The beauty of paradise exists not for its own sake but as a sadistic lure, designed to last just long enough to make one love it with all one's heart before being thrown out forever.

In *At the Bottom of the River*, Kincaid rewrote this punitive paradise, searching for a garden, but one not the creation of a power which demands that one yearn for that which one can never have. The collection's last, title story explores a dreamscape that seems to represent both the lost childhood and the lost Africa. Kincaid's paradise is not Milton's Eden, already the site of a power struggle. Rather, she creates a landscape where things exist for their own sakes, not yet having come to the attention of any power interests, not yet worked into any system of values that can then be used in a scheme of domination:

And in this world were many things blessed with unquestionable truth and purpose and beauty. There were steep mountains, there were valleys, there were seas, there were plains of grass, there were deserts, there were rivers, there were forests, there were vertebrates and invertebrates, there were mammals, there were reptiles, there were creatures of the dry land and the water, and there were birds. And they lived in this world not yet divided, not yet examined, not yet numbered, and not yet dead. I looked at this world as it revealed itself to me—how new, how new—and I longed to go there. (*BR*, 78)

In Kincaid's new story, creation is innocent, impartial, "unmindful of any of the individual needs of existence and without knowledge of future or past" (81). This vision allows the speaker finally to "emerge" from her "pit" (81), for if creation is impartial, there can be no mysterious original guilt. In the new story, one need not see oneself as Lucifer, eternally criminalized by creation, but as an innocent part of the innocent miracle of creation; one is able to join with creation, to see one's own existence as appropriately "perishable and transient" part of "all that is human endeavor. . . all that is past and . . . all that shall be, . . . all that shall be lost and leave no trace" (82).

In *Annie John*, paradise is once more a cruel trick; the mother's love is withdrawn, apparently because Annie begins, however inadvertently, to mature. Annie's sin is similar to Eve's; the first slight, unconscious step toward a sense of mature self is cause for violent expulsion by a power that will brook nothing but utter childlike innocence and ignorance. Annie's response is similar to Lucifer's. Although she has lost a paradise, she retains an "unconquerable will, / And study of revenge, immortal hate, / And courage never to submit or yield" (1.106–8). Thus, Annie teaches herself to scorn her once-adored mother, steal, lie, and do anything she knows her mother would hate. She takes up with the dirty and uncivilized Red Girl, and like Lucifer—who declares that "the mind is its own place, and in itself / Can make a Heaven of Hell, a Hell of Heaven" (1.254–55)—Annie now tries to make a heaven out of her outcast state. The paradise of the mother's world lost, she now declares the Red Girl's wild life a paradise: "She didn't like to go to Sunday school, and her mother didn't force her. She didn't like to brush her teeth, but occasionally her mother said it was necessary. She loved to play marbles, and was so good that only Skerritt boys now played against her. Oh, what an angel she was, and what a heaven she lived in!" (*AJ*, 58). But Annie's claim to make a heaven of her hell is mostly bravado; she finds she cannot sustain herself on revenge, and the joy goes out of her rebellions.

At the opening of the sixth chapter, "Somewhere, Belgium," Annie is plunged into a depression that has come upon her like a "mist," blotting out all the joy of life. Here Kincaid seems to divide her protagonist in two: the child part of Annie is the innocent Eve. The maturation process and its accompanying loss and depression, the blinding "mist," is Satan, who, in the form of a "black mist low-creeping," first makes his way into the Garden of Eden (9.180).

As Annie reaches her fifteenth birthday, the awkwardness and confusion of adolescence is so like a punishment that it seems to confirm the mother's view that Annie's loss of childhood is a kind of sin or perversion. In part, she is Eve, suddenly ashamed of her body: "My whole head was so big, and my eyes, which were big, too, sat in my big head wide open, as if I had just had a sudden fright. My skin was black in a way I had not noticed before. . . . On my forehead, on my cheeks were little bumps, each with a perfect, round white point. My plaits stuck out in every direction from under my hat; my long, thin neck stuck out from the blouse of my uniform" (*AJ*, 94).

But if Annie is in some ways still the innocent child, mysteriously taken over by evil, she also sees herself as evil incarnate. No longer is she the proud, rebellious Lucifer, as in the Red Girl section, but the Lucifer for whom "revenge, at first though sweet, / Bitter ere long back on itself recoils" (9.171–72). Now she sees herself as

> old and miserable. Not long before, I had seen a picture of a painting entitled *The Young Lucifer*. It showed Satan just recently cast out of heaven for all his bad deeds, and he was standing on a black rock all alone and naked. Everything around him was charred and black, as if a great fire had just roared through. His skin was coarse, and so were all his features. His hair was made up of live snakes, and they were in a position to strike. Satan was wearing a smile, but it was one of those smiles that you could see through, one of those smiles that makes you know the person is just putting up a good front. At heart, you could see, he was really lonely and miserable at the way things had turned out. (*AJ*, 94–95)

Annie spends most of the book identified with Satan, but by its end, the figure of Satan seems to have merged with the figure of Eve as Annie sadly departs paradise for a new world, one that is unknown but that she knows can never compare to her glorious Caribbean paradise.

In *Annie John*, Kincaid's protagonist identifies with the sympathetic Lucifer of the first books of *Paradise Lost*. In *At the Bottom of the River*, however, the Satan of the later books appears. Toward the end of Milton's work, Satan is transformed into a snake. Milton suggests that Satan is annually forced to undergo this "humbling . . . / To dash [the devil's] pride and joy for man seduced" (10.576–77). In *At the Bottom of the River* the figure who is thus transformed is the mother. But there is a difference between Milton's Satan and Kincaid's mother figure, in that for Satan, the transformation is involuntary and miserable:

> His visage drawn he felt to sharp and spare,
> His arms clung to his ribs, his legs entwining
> Each other, till, supplanted, down he fell
> A monstrous serpent on his belly prone. (10.511–14)

The mother's transformation to serpent is quite different. For her, the change is not a divine humiliation. On the contrary, it seems to be another demonstration of her power, something she accomplishes herself, carrying it out with the nonchalance of a woman preparing for bed: "She uncoiled her hair from her head and then removed her hair altogether. Taking her head into her large palms, she flattened it so that her eyes, which were by now ablaze, sat on top of her head and spun like two revolving balls. . . . Silently she had instructed me to follow her example, and now I too traveled along on my white underbelly, my tongue darting and flickering in the hot air" (*BR*, 55). At the end of the "Red Girl" chapter in *Annie John*, the mother is again associated with a serpent. Here, to win a battle over a cache of hidden marbles, the mother tells the story of how she was once, as a young girl, terrified by a snake that was hidden in a basket of figs. The story is calculated to inspire Annie's pity, to renew her love, and it does. Annie is on the verge of giving in and telling her mother where the marbles are hidden when she hears her mother's voice "warm and soft and treacherous" asking, "Well, Little Miss, where are your marbles?" (*AJ*, 70). Suddenly Annie understands that the story is an act of treachery and that the snake has been placed in the figs to induce her to betray herself.

   Throughout Kincaid's fiction the mother figure embodies power, whether as a condemning god or a seductive serpent. This pattern is continued in *Lucy*, where the title figure has been named for Lucifer by her mother. Pestered by the girl about the origin of the name, the mother finally replies, "I named you after Satan himself. Lucy, short for Lucifer. What a botheration from the moment you were conceived." Upon hearing this, the girl is delighted, going

> from feeling burdened and old and tired to feeling light, new, clean. I was transformed from failure to triumph. It was the moment I knew who I was. When I was quite young and just being taught to read, the books I was taught to read from were the Bible, *Paradise Lost*, and some plays by William Shakespeare. I knew well the Book of Genesis, and from time to time I had been made to memorize parts of *Paradise Lost*. The stories of the fallen were well known to me, but I had not known that my own situation could even distantly be related to them. Lucy, a girl's name for Lucifer. That my mother would have found me devil-like did not surprise me, for I often thought of her as god-like, and are not the children of gods devils? (*AJ*, 152–53)

If Lucy is Lucifer, her mother remains god, but here Lucifer, not God, seems to have won the great battle. Lucy, recently arrived in a North American city, has set up her own new world far from her mother's dominion. Although it is no paradise, especially in the cold, dead northeastern winter, she now finds herself to possess the kind of vision and control her mother had at home. Here, it seems, she may challenge the creator's power. Lucy, like the mother in *Annie John*, stands outside and above, able to see into other lives without being seen into. But though Lucy no longer seems to be obsessed by guilt or to ponder the question of the fall from grace, she cannot forget the lost glory or the all-powerful mother, "large, like a god . . . not an ordinary human being but something from an ancient book" (150). At the close of the book, however, Lucy has, to a certain extent, managed to escape the sway of her godlike mother and to come into her own powers. Kincaid's Lucifer, unlike Milton's, remains human and hopeful, if still waiting to find a life to go with her new freedom and power.

In the sixth chapter of *Annie John*, Annie begins to escape her increasingly oppressive surroundings by daydreaming. In her "most frequent" daydream she imagines herself living alone in Belgium, "a place I had picked when I read in one of my books that Charlotte Brontë, the author of my favorite novel, *Jane Eyre*, had spent a year or so there." In this daydream, Annie is far from her mother, who could only communicate by sending letters to "Somewhere, Belgium." Here Annie can be alone, adult, and wise, "walking down a street in Belgium, wearing a skirt that came down to my ankles and carrying a bag filled with books that at last I could understand" (*AJ*, 92).

It is not difficult to understand the affinity Kincaid has felt for Brontë or for Brontë's heroine, Jane Eyre, and to read *Annie John* and *Lucy* as a two-part bildungsroman is to observe many similarities in the predicament and progress of Brontë's heroine and of Kincaid's. Foremost among these is the sense of being constantly and unfairly put in the wrong by those whose interest is power, not justice. At the same time, an examination of Kincaid's and Brontë's works together points up in these two writers' views the difference between class oppression and oppression that stems from the ruptures of slavery and from colonialism. At the end of *Jane Eyre*, Jane not only triumphs utterly over her former oppressors, the Reeds, but also regains her lost birthright, so that she can become part of the class that once persecuted her. Jane's loss of birthright is a mistake that can be repaired, and once this is done, there is a place for her within the social organization. For Annie and Lucy, in contrast, injustice can never be completely overcome. Their birthright has not been mistakenly mislaid, as was Jane's, but purposely obliterated, and their rightful place can never be found.

Jane's struggle against an oppressive class system in nineteenth-century England has many parallels to the struggle of Annie and Lucy with an oppressive system based on class and race in twentieth-century Antigua and America. In both instances, the social and political oppression is echoed in the home lives of the young girls. In Annie's case, the mother's refusal to accept the girl's pending maturity mirrors the colonial society's refusal to recognize the mature humanity of those descended from slaves. In Jane's case, her persecution by the Reed family, rich relatives with whom the orphaned and impoverished girl lives, reflects nineteenth-century English society's castigation of those who cannot be placed within a rigid class system and who therefore are seen as challenging the system, however inadvertently. Jane, as one of the maids points out, does not even have the status of a servant who would, at least, have a secure place in the social organization:

> "For shame, for shame!" cried the lady's maid. "What shocking conduct, Miss Eyre, to strike a young gentleman, your benefactress' son! Your young master."
>
> "Master! How is he my master? Am I a servant?"
>
> "No; you are less than a servant, for you do nothing for your keep. There, sit down, and think over your wickedness." (44)

While both Jane Eyre and Annie John are virtually blameless, both are criminalized, Annie for beginning to mature in a racist society and Jane for failing to fit into a specific social class. In both works, the theme of rebellion is linked to that of enslavement. Kincaid gave Annie an awareness of her slave heritage, an awareness that is in itself something of a rebellion, since the colonial school system seeks to obscure the horror of slavery by treating that era as a heroic period of discovery. And Brontë, writing in 1847, likened Jane to a rebellious slave when she suddenly and without premeditation fights back against her "master." Jane muses, "I was conscious that a moment's mutiny had already rendered me liable to strange penalties, and, like any other rebel slave, I felt resolved, in my desperation, to go all lengths" (44). Both Jane and Annie come to see that the system under which they live is committed to their continued, psychic "enslavement," and further, that it is too powerful for any individual to fight. Both young women realize they will be locked into an inferior or subservient identity as long as they stay where they are; for both the only hope is to escape to a place where one might be seen for oneself.

In *Jane Eyre* and *Annie John*, the young girls are scapegoated by those who are clearly inferior to them. In both, the girls' tormentors are painted in distinctly unflattering terms; those who would dehumanize are seen as less than human. Brontë does not allow us to imagine that there is anything innately aristocratic about the Reeds. They are dishonest, bullying, self-pitying, and utterly unable to grasp that Jane, too, is a human being. They are, moreover, ugly. Fourteen-year-old John Reed, Jane's chief tormentor, is "large and stout for his age, with a dingy and unwholesome skin; thick lineaments in a spacious visage, heavy limbs and large extremities. He gorged himself habitually at table, which made him bilious, and gave him a dim and bleared eye with flabby cheeks" (41). In *Annie John* the teachers, the representatives of colonial power, are made petty and ridiculous. Like the Reeds, they have no redeeming features; they are as soulless as they are physically unattractive. Annie's headmistress, for instance, "looked like a prune left out of its jar a long time and she sounded as if she had borrowed her voice from an owl. The way she said, 'Now girls. . . ' When she was just standing still there, listening to some of the other activities, her gray eyes going all around the room hoping to see something wrong, her throat would beat up and down as if a fish fresh out of water were caught inside" (36).

Both Jane and Annie are aware that they are being treated with injustice and hypocrisy, and both have a sense of self that does not allow them to submit, even though they understand they will never have the power to prevail in their present circumstances. For both, the attempt to rebel brings on a crisis, for they are overwhelmed by the enormity of the forces allied against them. Jane defends herself against John Reed's unprovoked attack and, when she refuses to apologize, is locked into the majestically ghostly Red Room, where she goes into a fit of terror and falls unconscious. And Annie, struggling to rebel against forces at home and at school that would deny her true identity, is finally crushed by the weight of her opposition and falls into a long physical and mental illness.

Yet, for both Jane and Annie, it is this collapse that opens the way for escape. After Jane falls unconscious, a kindly chemist is called and, hearing how she has been treated, suggests that she be sent away to school, to which the cold and bitter Mrs. Reed agrees. Though Jane is not yet freed of class oppression, she has made a step; her rebellion has at least freed her of the Reeds' particular brand of subjugation. When Annie falls ill, it is her maternal grandmother, Ma Chess, who arrives and who, like the chemist in *Jane Eyre*, recognizes that the illness is one of the spirit. Although the chemist's mild intercession cannot be compared with Ma Chess's act of rebirthing, the two healers bring about similar results. In each case, a kindly, healing presence that acknowledges the girl's pain provides just enough help to allow her to survive and escape. Both young women, it seems, have threatened the forces aligned against them through the only means available to them; they are prepared to die of their ill treatment, and under this threat, relief has been provided.

Jane goes away to school, Lowood, and nurtured there by the kind, noble, and intellectual Miss Temple, she finds serenity. Miss Temple, like Ma Chess, remothers the girl, whose only previous experience with maternal nurture has been the harsh and grudging care of her aunt, Mrs. Reed, and the flippant attentions of the maid, Bessie. But eventually Miss Temple marries and goes away, and without her tranquilizing presence, Jane grows restless as her inner self demands definition. She begins to yearn for experience of the "wide" world and a "varied field of hopes and fears, of sensations and excitement," which she imagines await those who seek "real knowledge of life amidst its perils" (116). Jane then goes to the great estate Thornwood Hall, where she becomes governess for Mr. Rochester's charge, Adele, and is soon loved for her own virtuous and original self by the jaded Edward Rochester.

In *Annie John*, Kincaid's young protagonist also leaves for school. When next seen in *Lucy*, however, she has skipped school and gone directly to a position with a well-to-do family, taking care of children.

Here, like Jane at Thornwood Hall, Lucy is appreciated for her own deep and interesting self by her wealthy employer, Mariah, and the two become more like loving companions than like master and servant.

Although both Jane and Lucy are treated kindly and, to a great extent, as equals by their employers, they are still seen as mere servants by their employers' friends and, as such, not quite fully human. At a party, Mr. Rochester's guests do not hesitate to denigrate the entire governess class in tones loud enough for Jane to hear. When one of the group warns that Jane can hear the conversation, the woman speaking replies," 'I hope it may do her good!' Then, in a lower tone, but still loud enough for [Jane] to hear, 'I noticed her; I am a judge of physiognomy, and in hers I see all the faults of her class'" (206). And Lucy sees that to Mariah's friend Dinah, "someone in my position is 'the girl'—as in 'the girl who takes care of the children.' It would never have occurred to her that I had sized her up immediately, that I viewed her as a cliché, a something not to be, a something to rise above" (58).

Both young women perceive the perfectly turned-out rich people to be empty and posturing. Of Blanche Ingrim, the most brilliant of the aristocratic ladies to attend Mr. Rochester's house party, Jane Eyre says, "She was very showy, but she was not genuine; she had a fine person, many brilliant attainments, but her mind was poor, her heart barren by nature; nothing bloomed spontaneously on that soil; no unforced natural fruit delighted by its freshness. She was not good; she was not original: she used to repeat sounding phrases from books: she never offered, nor had, an opinion of her own" (215). And the wealthy friends of Lucy's employers remind the young woman of the mannequins in the catalogs she used to study as a child: "In the catalogue were pictures of clothes on mannequins, but the mannequins had no head or limbs, only torsos. I used to wonder what face would fit on the torso I was looking at, how such a face would look as it broke out in a smile, how it would look back at me if suddenly we were introduced. Now I knew, for these people, all standing there, holding drinks in their hands, reminded me of the catalogue; their clothes, their features, the manner in which they carried themselves were the examples all the world should copy" (64).

Even though both Brontë and Kincaid portray genuine affection between their young protagonists and the wealthy employers, both writers also cause the perfect exterior of the employers' lives to crumble, revealing a tangle of perfidy and pain. In Brontë's work, Jane is the unwitting agent of these revelations. It is Jane's capture of Rochester's heart and his desire to marry her that brings the fact of his disastrous previous marriage to light. Further, Rochester's attachment to Jane apparently causes Bertha, Rochester's mad first wife who is kept imprisoned in the attic, to set the fire that destroys Rochester's estate and costs him the use of his arm and eyes. Fiction gives Brontë the luxury of allowing Jane to retain her innocence even as she takes revenge against the class that has oppressed her. In Kincaid's work, Lucy does not cause the disruption of her employers' family, but she does see what the family tries to keep hidden. In spite of skilled manipulation of appearances, she sees that Mariah's husband is unfaithful and that the family is breaking apart.

While Jane is, however inadvertently, the agent of Rochester's loss of power and control, Lucy does not cause Mariah and Lewis's family life to crumble. But Kincaid did give her protagonist another way of taking power from the powerful, and in this, we begin to see that while there are similarities between the worlds that Brontë and Kincaid depict, there are also profound differences. In Brontë's world, all the youthful heroine finally needs is her honesty and innocence, and when this is introduced into the corrupt world of Rochester and fashionable society, that world must fall, evil deeds must be revealed, houses burned, and strong men maimed. Brontë saw social injustice realistically, but envisioned a solution only through the gauze of fairy-tale magic. In *Lucy* the reverse is true, for Kincaid saw the assumed superiority of Lewis and Mariah as a fairy tale they tell about themselves, something she could combat only by cutting through the gauze to the real picture below. For Brontë, a fairy tale is the solution, used to lift the powerless. In Kincaid's world, where the most magical story is that of the brilliant and eternal superiority of the British over their colonized peoples, the fairy tale is the problem, holding the powerless down.

Thus, while Brontë empowers Jane by constructing a fairy tale, Kincaid empowers Lucy by deconstructing one. Lucy's revenge is, first, to see behind the perfect facade of Mariah and Lewis's life and, second, to show that she has seen. Lucy grasps that Lewis is unfaithful long before Mariah does, and when the rupture finally does come, Lucy is there to observe and record it. Arriving home one day after taking the children to the park, Lucy sees Mariah and Lewis talking. She sees that Mariah has been crying, though she is now trying to smile bravely, and Lucy knows the end has come. Lucy takes out her camera, which she now carries with her everywhere, and "for a reason that will never be known to me, I said, 'Say, "cheese"' and took a picture. Lewis said, 'Jesus Christ,' and he left our company in anger" (118). While Kincaid does not literally cause the house to burn and the master to be maimed, she destroys the assumed moral superiority of the privileged by seeing and recording the confusion behind the picture-perfect facade constructed by the privileged.

As both books move toward their resolutions, the different world-views of Brontë and Kincaid become even more apparent, though the actions of Jane and Lucy are, on the surface, similar. Both, though befriended and even beloved by their employers, must strike out on their own if they are ever to find themselves. Both realize that in these relationships, however loving, they are still dependent and that the terms of their lives are still being determined by someone else.

In *Jane Eyre* this potential state of dependency is taken to extremes when Jane, as she prepares to marry Rochester, finds that he already has a wife and that she can only be his mistress. If she were to marry him, she would be without any legal or moral place within the established order, entirely dependent on his whim. Over Rochester's furious protests, Jane flees to a place where she knows no one. As she alights there she says simply, "I am alone" (349). We realize that though we have seen Jane friendless, we have not before seen her alone. She wanders destitute on the heath, close to death from cold and starvation, consciously choosing this fate over a luxurious life of dependence. But, as if tested by this ordeal and found worthy, her fortunes are suddenly reversed. The door on which she knocks as she is about to expire turns out to be, after much confusion, that of her lost family—an "ancient" and genteel lineage. A timely inheritance makes her rich. Now, with her own social and financial power, she is able to return to Rochester as an equal.

Lucy, too, decides to leave a comfortable home, over her employer's protests, and at last finds herself alone, free of the relationships that have always been based, however subtly, on power. She, like Jane, is looking for something, but also like Jane, she will not know what it is until she finds it. Lucy is not literally starving to death in a wilderness, as Jane is, but she has succeeded in cutting herself off from everything familiar. Having left her mother and her West Indian home, having left Mariah and the luxurious surroundings of wealth, Lucy moves into a small apartment, free as long as she can come up with the rent. Lucy's solitude, like Jane's, is heroic, not euphoric. "I was alone in the world," she says. "It was not a small accomplishment. I thought I would die doing it" (161).

Both young women must leave their comfortable surroundings in order to undergo a solitary ordeal, but the results of these two ordeals are profoundly different. Jane Eyre's flight into the unknown is the last step taken before what turns out to be a rather simple mistake is corrected. Her mislaid birthright is recovered; she is allowed to take her rightful place in society. Now she may return to Rochester as an equal and presumably live happily ever after as his wife. Lucy's story, on the other hand, ends in solitary ordeal. And while Kincaid may not yet be finished with her bildungsroman, it seems unlikely that her protagonist will be able to recover so thoroughly what has been lost and to place herself so firmly within a once-hostile society, as does Jane Eyre. Finally, Brontë's "rebel slave" does not rebel against the class system that persecutes and criminalizes the innocent but against her own mistaken placement in that system. Indeed, as Jane's condescending attitude toward servants and the rough country girls who are her students shows, she herself believes in the innate superiority of the genteel. Once Jane has recovered family and fortune, once she can enter the gentility as an equal, she is content; the problem of oppression has been solved. Brontë's heroine, it turns out, merely seemed to be trapped between two worlds. In fact, she has always known that she belongs in the ruling class, and in the best fairy-tale tradition, Jane, after surviving certain ordeals, is transformed from slave to master, as all acknowledge that a mistake has been made.

But for Kincaid's protagonists there can be no such simple resolution. Annie and Lucy could never, by a reversal of personal fortune, take their rightful place in society, for rightful society itself has been lost, and Annie and Lucy are truly trapped between worlds. They will never be fully African, nor will they ever be fully Westernized. They can never be magically transformed from rebel slave to master, for to do so, they would have to endorse the physical and psychological violence committed against them, not, as in Jane Eyre, against some mistaken apprehension of them. To achieve union with the dominant group, they would be required not only to approve the theft of land, culture, and language but also to applaud its continued profit as a result of these thefts. The oppression of Annie and Lucy is the result not of temporarily misplaced information concerning important connections but of connections irreversibly severed.

Kincaid's interest in Jane Eyre, the similarity of themes in Brontë's work and in Kincaid's, then the sudden divergence as Brontë veers off into a happy ending unavailable to Kincaid, all seem to demonstrate, among other things, the difference between class oppression and the oppression that springs from the crime of slavery. In Brontë's world, wrongs can conceivably be righted; in Kincaid's, they cannot. As Lucy draws to a close, Kincaid's protagonist comes less and less to resemble the Cinderella-like Jane Eyre, more and more to resemble Bertha Mason, Rochester's first wife, the dark West Indian woman whom he married for her money, who is drawn to him because he is "of a good race" (332), who is found to be "intemperate and unchaste" (334), who is pronounced insane and imprisoned forever. Bertha, a mad presence in Rochester's attic, is the secret cause of his dissipations, self-loathing, and inability to find true happiness. While Bertha is presented by Brontë as mad and violent, the opposite of the controlled and proper Jane, she can also be understood as Jane's "truest darkest double: she is the angry aspect of the orphan child, the ferocious secret self Jane [tries] to repress."[3] Further, she can be read as the tortured human evidence of colonial activity, as the "'dark' secret, the maddening burden of imperialism concealed in the heart of every English gentleman's house of the time."[4]

The angry and somewhat distant Lucy, who explodes fairy tales, can be read as the "ferocious secret self" of the early, yearning Annie, a girl who still hoped for magical solutions to her problems through a Brontë-style escape to "Somewhere, Belgium." Lucy, like Bertha, is a "burden of imperialism" who cannot be gotten rid of, destroying Mariah's pleasure in the daffodils by demonstrating how these seemingly innocent flowers were used as a tool of colonial oppression, grasping, even if Mariah does not, the connection between the comforts of privilege and "the decline of the world that lay before them" (72). Lucy sees through the desire to cleanse history by rinsing it with romance. She understands that her lover, Paul, is fascinated by her in part because "he loved ruins; he loved the past but only if it ended on a sad note, from a lofty beginning to a gradual, rotten decline" (156). She dismays Mariah by not being gratified when Mariah confides that she has some Indian blood, "as if she were announcing her possession of a trophy" (40). Lucy sees that the privileged Mariah, whose Great Lakes summer home was probably once the home of others with Indian blood, has so thoroughly internalized her right to have what she wants that she feels perfectly innocent and unthreatened and so can easily afford the exotic luxury of identifying with those at whose expense her privilege has been bought. Like Bertha, who always manages to escape her attic prison at just the right moment to upset Rochester's plans to proceed as if she does not exist, Lucy is always there, refusing to allow her history to be either ignored or romanticized.

Kincaid's two autobiographical novels, in their very similarity to Brontë's bildungsroman and Milton's creation epic, engage these canonical works in a dialogue on power and oppression. Rather than ignoring the part of her heritage that includes Charlotte Brontë and John Milton, rather than allowing her own story to be misshaped by literary traditions of a culture that was never her own, Kincaid has, to use Françoise Lionnet's phrase, "interact[ed] on an equal footing with . . . the traditions that determine [her] present predicament" (7). If we read *Annie John* and *Lucy* as rewritings of *Jane Eyre*, we can see Kincaid setting out the difference between the kind of oppression Jane suffers and the kind experienced by Annie and Lucy. Kincaid's Lucy asks her friend Mariah, "How do you get to be the sort of victor who can claim to be the vanquished also?" (41). We can imagine Kincaid asking Brontë something similar: How can your vision of justice be at once so inflamed and so limited?

Chapter Six

At the Bottom of the River: Journey of Mourning

The ten dreamlike stories that make up *At the Bottom of the River* are the most difficult of all Kincaid's works to date. Speakers go unidentified, identities merge, fantasy and reality are inseparable. Critics have wondered whether the stories are finally "too personal and too peculiar to translate into any sort of sensible communication" (E. Milton, 22). But, if taken together and read in the context of Kincaid's other work, the pieces cannot be dismissed as brilliant but indecipherable dreamscapes. Rather, the ten pieces trace an emotional journey, a journey of mourning. What is mourned is the loss of a prelapsarian world, a childhood paradise of perfect love and harmony in which time stands still and in which betrayal—including the great betrayal of death—is unknown.

As the ten pieces move through the stages of mourning—from denial, through anger and depression, to a vision of peaceful acceptance—they seem to fall into three groups. The first four stories, "Girl," "In the Night," "At Last," and "Wingless," deny the permanence of the loss but seek a way of going back, of being once again the child, the infant or even the fetus in the womb, "swim[ming] in a shaft of light, upside down" (21).

The next group, "Holidays," "The Letter from Home," and "What I Have Been Doing Lately," are told from the perspective of one who has left the childhood world but is still in limbo, recording a collection of sensations that do not quite add up. In "What I Have Been Doing Lately," for example, a dream journey seems to entrap the narrator in an endless cycle of departure, yearning, and awareness of the impossibility of return.

In the final group of stories, "Blackness," "My Mother," and "At the Bottom of the River," the narrator squarely faces the crisis of loss, feeling herself to have been erased, silenced, numbed. This feeling, similar to the crisis in *Annie John*, is experienced as a "blackness" that silently falls all around, soft and dense as soot. In "My Mother" the narrator begins her actual journey of departure, leaving a mother, then finding what appears to be another mother, one with whom there is a sense of openness, of fertility, of a future, of "rooms [that] are large and empty, opening on to each other, waiting for people and things to fill them up" (60). In "At the Bottom of the River," the narrator manages to replace the lost perfection of childhood love and innocence with another, more mature joy in her understanding of the impartiality and implacability of creation, a force "unmindful of any of the individual needs of existence, and without knowledge of future or past" (81). Creation is still innocent, timeless, perfectly itself; whatever one's personal loss, one may still see oneself as a part of this creation. Though one vision of light and beauty has been lost, another has been found. With this, Kincaid's narrator may move on into maturity and her own life; she may "emerge" from the "pit," "step into a room and . . . see that the lamp is lit," and she may feel her own name "filling up [her] mouth" (81–82).

In her first published *New Yorker* fiction, "Girl," the story with which she felt she found her voice as a writer, Jamaica Kincaid presented a microcosm of her future themes and concerns. This intense, one-sentence, three-page story both celebrates and abhors the beauty and power of her childhood world, demonstrating why its pull is so strong, why that pull must be resisted, and why the sense of its loss is so powerful. Here, too, the world of obeah magic is introduced, coexisting easily with the domestic domains of kitchen and market.

The most striking aspect of the piece is its voice, the voice of a mother instructing her daughter and, in doing so, describing a world. The story is not a transcript of actual remarks, though the opening, with its specific advice, gives the impression of literally recorded speech: "Wash the white clothes on Monday and put them on the stone heap; wash the color clothes on Tuesday and put them on the clothesline to dry . . ." (3). As soon as we take this impression, Kincaid alters the terms ever so slightly, repeatedly beginning her phrases with "This is how you . . ." (4). The mother still seems to be speaking of how to do things, and the reader barely notices that she is no longer actually giving specific advice. This change allows Kincaid to widen imperceptibly the scope of the mother's remarks, until they are finally seen to be not simple household advice at all but a litany of protection and control, a chant that sounds the need for constant alertness to, and study of, one's surroundings. Implied here is the conviction that such alertness is the only defense against a magically dangerous world in which "something bad" might always "fall on you" (5).

This is a voice that needs no help, no introductory "As my mother always said," no explanatory quotation marks. It is a voice so sure of itself and its power to control that it does not deign to explain itself in any way. Rather, with the first lines we feel that we are picking up remarks in progress, that there is no beginning. It is a voice that does not pause or explain, but moves by its own logic, holding the reader with its repetitive and rhythmic patterns. It is not a voice to which one effectively speaks back—as the two italicized attempts at response make clear—and we realize that this is not merely the mother's voice, but the mother's mesmerizing rhythm of life and knowledge, power and protection, as internalized by the daughter.

This voice represents the energy and life of the childhood world and reveals why it is not a world in which the daughter may remain if she wishes to grow into her own power, for the all-powerful voice of maternal nurture and knowledge is also the voice of condemnation and threat. The positive and negative currents are so intermixed that it is nearly impossible to detect the moment at which one merges into the other. From the apparently benevolent advice on how to buy material for a blouse and how to cook fish, the voice turns to "Is it true that you sing benna [a folk song] in Sunday school?" (3). This is a change, but it is still easily within the context of loving maternal interest, as is the next remark, though we may register a negative shading: "Always eat your food in such a way that it won't turn someone else's stomach." We feel ourselves on solid ground with the next remark, "on Sundays try to walk like a lady," only to be slammed into the ugly accusation "and not like the slut you are so bent on becoming" (3).

Where did benevolence turn to attack? Where, exactly, should we have put up our guard? With the suggestion that the girl eats in a disgusting way? With the question about the inappropriate singing of benna? Or even earlier, with the advice to immediately soak "little cloths," which hints of menstrual blood, the onset of physical maturation, and thus the possibility of sluttishness? Reeling, as the girl is reeling, from the whipsaw effect of the mother's advice, we now read, "Don't sing benna in Sunday school; you mustn't speak to wharf-rat boys, not even to give directions" (3). Does she sing benna? Does she speak to wharf-rat boys? Whether she does or not, she stands condemned. But any such protest is answered by the mother's next remark, which shows that, in her view, innocence and degradation fit effortlessly together: "Don't eat fruits on the street—flies will follow you" (3–4).

At this point the daughter manages to answer back, in the italicized, *"But I don't sing benna on Sundays at all and never in Sunday school"* (4). It is a feeble protest, which the mother does not even acknowledge. Perhaps she only thinks these words, for the mother's voice chants on about sewing, buttons and buttonholes, only to use this apparently innocuous theme as a route back to the accusation of sluttishness: "This is how to hem a dress when you see the hem coming down and so to prevent yourself from looking like the slut I know you are so bent on becoming" (4).

Nurture and attack are here inseparable; one always masquerades as the other, turns into the other. And now, around line 25, nurture itself becomes dangerous. The advice still has to do with household matters, but it is becoming increasingly clear that the efficient housekeeper must manage far more than the laundry and the shopping. She must know how to control and manipulate ("This is how you smile to someone you don't like too much; this is how you smile to someone you don't like at all" [4]), and she must be aware that nothing is ever what it seems, that dangerous magic is to be guarded against everywhere: "Don't pick people's flowers— you might catch something; don't throw stones at blackbirds, because it might not be a blackbird at all . . ." (5). Ultimately, the mother's own homely tasks are themselves seen as veering into the dangerously magical. Her recipes range from bread pudding to medicine for a cold to "medicine to throw away a child before it even becomes a child" (5).

What is finally being taught in this maternal litany is that the world is full of masked dangers and that one of these dangers is the maternal voice itself. The story demonstrates the power of that voice, its mesmerizing, manipulative intensity, and shows the daughter's near helplessness before the voice. After the first feeble reply, she is silent until the end of the story when she makes a remark that the mother does respond to, but only, it seems, because the girl's words can be used to incriminate her. When the mother, moving effortlessly from deadly magic to grocery shopping, advises squeezing the bread to make sure that it is fresh, the girl asks, "But what if the baker won't let me feel the bread?" This time the mother does respond to her remark, as if perversely reminded of the earlier theme of sluttishness by the daughter's very innocence: "You mean to say that after all you are really going to be the kind of woman who the baker won't let near the bread?" (5).

In this story, Kincaid's "girl" is still a child, paralyzed by the mesmerizing maternal voice, fascinated by its power, capable of only the weakest protest when unfair assumptions are made about her. Her world has not yet been lost; rather, it must be lost if the girl is to mature, to find a voice beyond the faint squeak of self-defense heard here.

In the collection's second story, "In the Night," Kincaid moves from the relatively realistic, daylight world of "Girl" to the dark middle of the night, a dimension that does not follow the rules of daytime life but rather the irrational movements of the unconscious. This place, governed by the unknowable laws of obeah magic, is timeless and without recognizable shape, "round in some places, flat in some places, and in some places like a deep hole" (6). In "Girl," magical powers and forces must be detected behind the prosaic fabric of the mother's remarks; in this second story, the reader is plunged into a dark world of mysterious forces. Confronted directly with mystery, the girl's power seems to shrink even more. First, she is an infant, helpless as a lamb, but by the story's end, she has returned in fantasy to the womb, listening every night to a story told by her mother "that begins, 'Before you were born'" (12). In this story, more than in any other, we see Kincaid's protagonist struggle to hold onto her childhood world, even if it means her own infantilization.

In the first section of "In the Night" Kincaid shows what we see when we look behind the daylight facade of rationality. Though there are men and women in this world, the men only look on, like the nightsoil men, who see but remain silent. Males are innocuous, even a walking dead man like Mr. Gishard, who returns to haunt the place where he lived but who is mild, harmless, even a little foolish, wearing a nice white suit and missing his accordion. The women, in contrast, take advantage of the magical possibilities. One, a woman who is "reasonable" by day, appreciating pleasant and tranquil things, has in the night removed her skin and turned herself into a bird. She is glimpsed "on her way to drink the blood of her secret enemies" (6). Another woman comes back from the dead, but unlike the mild, bemused Mr. Gishard, she returns to torment the living.

In the story's second section, we see that the narrator's mother is one of the women who use the night to work changes. As the mother can change wet sheets for dry ones, she "can change everything," including, she hints to the girl, herself, for the mother is young and beautiful, and the "jablesse" in the mountains, with its eyes like lamps, always "tries to look like a beautiful woman" (9). The girl, too, changes in the night, but rather than taking on added powers and forbidden knowledge, she becomes even more innocent and helpless, unable to control even bodily functions. She dreams of a baby being born and then becomes the baby, innocent as a lamb, "eating green grass with its soft and pink lips" (8), awakening from the dream to find that she has wet the bed.

Nothing can be relied on in the magical world behind daylight reality. It cannot be described by stories of simple happiness and stable character. This is demonstrated by the story's third section, which begins, "No one has ever said to me" (9), and proceeds with a long paragraph detailing the mild, reasonable, and kind manner of "my father, a nightsoil man" (9), who "makes us happy" and who "has promised that one day he will take us to see something he has read about called the circus" (10). The night, Kincaid seems to say, is the real world behind appearances. It is the opposite of the world represented by mild fathers who want to treat their families to a circus.

The night, as the story's fourth section shows, is a place where even nature is anxious, as the "flowers close up and thicken" (10) and are "vexed" (11). It is a place where simple, quiet activities may veer into silent murder as "someone is sprinkling a colorless powder outside a closed door so that someone else's child will be stillborn" (11).

Then, as if in frightened retreat from this world of dark powers, the protagonist constructs an elaborate child's picture of love and safety, a fantasy in which she "marries" a woman like her mother, "who wears skirts that are so big I can easily bury my head in them" (11). They will live together in a hut by the sea with a simple, satisfying collection of household utensils. They will be mother and daughter, but they will also be children together, climbing trees, stealing fruit. Though the mother "knows many things," she will never allow her knowledge and power to hurt the child. Instead, she will treat the child as if she were still part of the mother's self, telling "every night, over and over" a story "that begins, 'Before you were born.'" Then—and Kincaid seems to say only then, only in a return to the womb—can the girl be "completely happy" (12). Such a return is of course impossible, as is recognized even within this fantasy, for one of the household items in the mud hut by the sea is a picture of two women standing on a jetty embracing and waving good-bye, and as readers of *Annie John* will know, this picture, which foreshadows a girl's permanent departure from her mother and her home, suggests not eternal union but irreversible separation.

In the first section of the story "At Last," entitled "The House," we encounter another version of the mother-daughter dialogue of "Girl." Here, the daughter asks the mother about their life together in a time before the girl can remember. Kincaid's protagonist is still obsessed with the world of her childhood and the relation between her mother and herself. Her interrogation of the mother seems to be another ploy, like the fantasy of marrying her mother in the previous story, to fix and hold the childhood world. Here, too, as the voices cannot always be distinguished one from another and at times seem to meld, we see Kincaid merging the protagonist with the mother as a way of avoiding the inevitable rupture. But, as in the previous story, the fantasy of perfect union, even as it might exist in memory, cannot be achieved. The recollection of domestic life—"I lived in this house with you; the wood shingles, unpainted, weather-beaten, fraying; the piano, a piece of furniture now, collecting dust; the bed in which all the children were born" (13)—veers immediately into death, loss, and unknowability. There are flowers, "alive, then dead," and there was a bowl of fruit, "but then all eaten." The hair brush is "full of dead hair," and letters bring bad news (13).

Things seem to crumble the moment they are addressed. In the same way, the speaker cannot trust the one to whom she is speaking to remember things correctly or even to be who she claims to be: "What are you now? A young woman. But what are you really?" (13). Over and over, these questions are asked as the speaker, who seems to be the daughter, tries to fix the memory of the past. Again and again, the mother answers elusively, or the questions trigger her own train of thought, which finally works to undercut the memory world the daughter is trying to create: "What passed between us then? You asked me if it was always the way it is now. But I don't know. I wasn't always here. I wasn't here in the beginning. We held hands once and were beautiful. But what followed? Sleepless nights, oh, sleepless nights" (14). In another passage the daughter's question "So I was loved?" triggers this ambiguous response: "Yes. You wore your clothes wrapped tight around your body, keeping your warmth to yourself. What greed!" (16).

Toward the end of this section, we sense, as we do in the second half of "Girl," a change in the mother's voice as it moves from controlled, manipulative responses, to responses that indicate a self veering out of rational control and escaping into another dimension where it is free and strong. While both "Girl" and "At Last" are, on one level, about the daughter and her seeming helplessness in her interaction with this powerful mother, on another level these pieces are about the mother and her ability to transform herself into something wild and fearless: "I wore blue, bird blue, and at night I would shine in the dark," and, "Sometimes I appeared as a hoofed animal, stroking my own brown, shiny back. Then I left no corner unturned. Nothing frightened me" (17).

The daughter's questions are punctuated throughout this section by a question about "the light." Set off in parentheses, this question is asked four times with no response: "(What was that light?)," "(Was that the light again?)" (13), "(But the light, where does it come from, the light?)" (14), "(It's the light again, now in flashes)" (15). We do not know what this light is; possibly it is the love the daughter seeks to recover, the light that can illuminate the darkness of loss. Possibly it is the mother's brilliance, which in the previous story is related to the eyes of the jablesse, shining like lamps.

In the last paragraphs of this section, however, the question finds a response, one that suggests that the effort to regain the past by remembering its details will always fail, that these details are nothing without the illumination of life and love. Here the voices of mother and daughter seem to blend; either could be speaking. We know that both mother and daughter in Kincaid's work take a solitary sea journey, the mother to Antigua from her childhood home in Dominica and the daughter, Annie, from Antigua to Britain. And we know that the protagonist in *At the Bottom of the River* is in search of a name that finally fills up her mouth in the book's last line. Perhaps we may see that both mother and daughter seek to regain what has been lost through an obsession with listing and measuring, but that, finally, this is a useless exercise if the light of love and life is gone:

> I crossed the open sea alone at night on a steamer. What was my name—
> I mean the name my mother gave to me—and where did I come from?
> My skin is now coarse. What pity. What sorrow. I have made a list. I
> have measured everything. I have not lied.
>   But the light. What of the light?
>   Splintered. Died. (17)

In the second section of "At Last," entitled "The Yard," the attempt to fix a picture of life by studying its domestic and emotional furniture is abandoned. Rather, the narrative moves to the out-of-doors, where it considers the impartial details and passionless struggles of nature. Here is "a mountain. A valley. The shade. The sun. A streak of yellow rapidly conquering a streak of green. Blending and separating" (17). Here "nothing is measured," and correspondingly, there is no sense of loss. An ant, walking on a sheet of tin in the sun, "crumbles" but it does not matter; "what is an ant?" (18). Humans may intrude upon this world with their plans and desires; someone has made a stone enclosure and planted bluebells for a child's garden. But here one expects human works to be undone. The bluebells will fall to the ground, but that is only part of a natural cycle, "dying and living in perpetuity."

For a time, this seems to be a solution. Change and death can be accepted as natural: "But what is a beetle? What is one fly? What is one day? What is anything after it is dead and gone? Another beetle will pause, sensing the danger. Another day, identical to this day . . . then the rain, beating the underbrush hard, causing the turtle to bury its head even more carefully. The stillness comes and the stillness goes. The sun. The moon" (19). But human voices are still heard, reminiscing about a child's game, a game that is itself about remembering and about lost worlds: "What was the song they used to sing and made fists and pretended to be Romans?" (19). Finally, Kincaid does not manage to ameliorate human loss by linking it to the inevitable cycle of nature.

In Kincaid's fourth story, "Wingless," the child moves out into the world, to school, to the sea, putting some small distance between herself and the domestic universe of the mother. This is the beginning of her effort to find a place for herself outside her mother's stronghold. And while this movement shows the girl awakening from the trance of the first three pieces to envision herself as a separate person, it also shows that this will not be an easy transition. At the same time that she begins to feel the possibility of change, of "discovery" (24), she is overwhelmed by a sense of her own fears and imperfections, still caught in a suffocating embrace with "the woman I love, who is so much bigger than me" (27). While the girl must "discover" herself, this task is complicated by the understanding that she is many contradictory things. In the story's final section, Kincaid returns, as she did in "At Last," to an examination of the natural world, as if, despairing of ever mastering the variables of human life, she tries to learn by studying the simpler progress of the mosquito, the ant, the land crab, and the butterfly. But what she notices about all of these lively creatures is that they are soon stilled, and once again, though she begins with a sense of becoming, Kincaid's protagonist reverts to her obsession with loss. Every effort, it seems, even the struggle to discover oneself, leads to the awareness of this loss, for, as the lively insect is silenced, so, in the final lines, is the girl, in a sleep that prefigures death. Kincaid's protagonist is no longer content to exist in a timeless child's world, as in "Girl," or to fantasize the impossible return to this world, as in "In the Night." But she is not yet able to envision separation as anything but death.

The girl knows that she, although still "wingless," is "on the brink" of something, and she sees herself as an unborn child, still in the womb but illuminated with possibility: "I swim in a shaft of light, upside down, and I can see myself clearly, through and through, from every angle" (24). But what, the first section asks, is she becoming? What is she discovering? Will her discoveries resemble those of Columbus, a figure ever in the mind of Caribbean and colonial children, as we will see in *Annie John*? Will she aspire to greatness and suffer for her ambition, being "sent home in chains" from the site of her discovery? Will her life be "as predictable as an insect's?" (21). Will she "grow up to be a tall, graceful, and altogether beautiful woman" and "impose" her will and "great pain" on "large numbers of people" for her own "amusement" (22)? Again, will her life be "like an apprenticeship in dressmaking, a thorny path to carefully follow or avoid?" (23).

The girl is determined to make sense of all the change and possibility: "I shall try to see clearly. I shall try to tell differences" (22). And she begins to evaluate everything, from the "subtle gradations of color in fine cloth" (22) to the question of whether her mother loves her and the question of who is worthy of being a best friend. She will try to control all the variables by listing them, treating them like physical items that can be counted and arranged: "I shall try to separate and divide things as if they were sums, as if they were drygoods on the grocer's shelves" (22).

But as she begins to list the elements of her life, the accounting of her own fears, faults, and griefs overwhelms her, drowning out the hope of possibilities: "My charm is limited, and I haven't learned to smile yet. I have picked many flowers and then deliberately torn them to shreds, petal by petal. I am so unhappy, my face is so wet, and still I can stand up and walk and tell lies in the face of terrible punishments" (23). She must, then, if disappointment is what she most possesses, learn to "cherish [her] disappointments" (24), to "pin tags on them" as if they were "newly domesticated animals" (23–24).

At the end of this section, in a passage that looks forward to "The Long Rain" section of *Annie John*, the girl seems overwhelmed by her attempt to separate herself from her mother and her mother's world. As Annie is immobilized during a torrential storm, "bolted . . . down" by the ceaseless thud of rain on the roof (*AJ*, 109), the protagonist in "Wingless" collects water in her body, immobilized by visions of the fearsome future that will arrive once the break she struggles to make is accomplished: "For days my body has been collecting water, but still I won't cry. What is that to me? I am not yet a woman with a terrible and unwanted burden. I am not yet a dog with a cruel and unloving master. I am not yet a tree growing in barren and bitter land. I am not yet the shape of darkness in a dungeon" (24).

In section two, the protagonist seems to retreat from her "brink of great discovery" (24) to a renewed obsession with the dark, mesmerizing power of the mother. Here the mother is shown delivering a piece of advice in a way reminiscent of the litany of admonitions delivered in "Girl." She advises, "Don't eat the strings on bananas—they will wrap around your heart and kill you." The girl believes this and is afraid she will die. She tries to remove the strings and is then mocked by the mother for her belief and fright, both of which the mother has carelessly inflicted (24).

In the third section, the mother is presented in a fantastic tableau, seen as holding a dark, magical sway over men. And in the fourth section this theme of omnipotence is continued as female power comes to be symbolized by the sea. Kincaid made this connection clear in her early short story "Antigua Crossing," in which she wrote, "The Caribbean Sea is so big, and so blue, and so deep, and so warm, and so unpredictable, and so inviting and so dangerous, and so beautiful. This is exactly the way I feel about all the women in my own family" (48). In "Wingless" the sea is "the blue, the green, the black, so deep, so smooth, a great and swift undercurrent, glassy, the white wavelets, a storm so blinding that the salt got in our eyes, the sea turning inside out, shaking everything up like a bottle with sediment" (25–26). At the end of the passage, "the sea [follows the speaker] home, snapping at my heels, all the way to the door, the sea, the woman" (26).

And then, as if demoralized by the vision of herself always smaller and weaker than her beloved antagonist, the speaker, as she often does at moments of stress, turns for help to the natural world. Yet, here again, life, however lively, comes to an end as the creatures—the nimble lizard, the sluggish ant, the contented butterfly—grow inevitably "so still" (27). Like nature, the girl is both cruel and innocent, and she, too, is "stilled" at the end of the story as sleep mocks death. Though she seeks a great liberating "discovery," she is left here with the frightful suspicion that liberation and separation can mean only death.

"Holidays," "Letter from Home," and "What I Have Been Doing" represent a departure from the previous four stories. With "Holidays," Kincaid's protagonist has left the dense and magical mother's world of the Caribbean and now floats somewhat aimlessly in a new environment. Wandering in pleasant but empty surroundings, the speaker seems to be on holiday not only from affairs in a North American city (probably New York) but from the passionate concerns of her own inner life as portrayed in the prior stories. The holiday resembles the peach the speaker considers going to buy at the village store: it will have a nice appearance and be warm "from sitting in a box in the sun" (30) and it will offer superficial comfort. But the peach—produced for looks and shelflife rather than flavor—is tasteless, and the speaker "will know that [she is] eating a peach only by looking at it" (30).

Kincaid's protagonist has made her escape from the mother's world, but cut off from everything she knows, she seems unable to exist fully, to focus, to know what she is feeling, even to know whether she wants a hot drink or a cold one. The protagonist seems to have lost touch with her own "taste," a sense of her own essence, and she tries to examine and record her sensations and appearance to gain some recognition of herself. So the story begins with a list of the minutiae of an aimless half-hour alone in what appears to be a holiday house in the mountains. The protagonist looks around the house, sees some flies, scratches herself, sighs, looks at a picture of butterflies in a book, puts her toe into dead fireplace ashes, then rubs it on the carpet. Finally, she examines herself as she might examine the oddly lifeless peach: "I am the only person sitting on the porch. I look at myself. I can see myself. That is, I can see my chest, my abdomen, my legs, and my arms. I cannot see my hair, my ears, my face, or my collarbone. I can feel them, though. My nose is moist with sweat. Locking my fingers, I put my hands on my head" (31).

This strategy for self-recovery seems to work, perhaps too well, for in rediscovering herself she inevitably calls up thoughts of her mother and the mother's magical world. Now the protagonist notices a large bee, "flying around aimlessly" (31), and we remember the blackbird in "Girl," who "might not be a blackbird at all" (5). We know from *Lucy* that in the mother's world, "when someone wanted to harm someone else they sent the harm in the shape of an animal" (151). The bee, then, the first moving thing in the story so far, might not be a bee at all. Whatever it is, even if it is only a bee, its appearance reminds the protagonist of her mother and the world at home. She takes her hands from her head because they are tired but "also because I have just remembered a superstition: if you sit with your hands on your head, you will kill your mother" (31). Returned to the mother's world, she feels both the near-murderous passion she and her mother share, as well as her own abiding sense of guilt.

The protagonist now considers writing a letter to someone, addressed as "Dear So-and-So." As is clear in *Lucy* and other writings, such as "Jamaica Kincaid's New York," the topic of letters almost always has to do with a communication between mother and daughter, a communication fraught with loss, guilt, deception, and anger. In *Lucy* the girl saves, but does not open, her mother's letters and never writes back (91). Here the imagined letter strings together boastful clichés of conquest: ". . . and then I got the brilliant idea . . . I was very amusing" (31). But cliché cannot entirely protect one from revealing actual feelings, and a new set of clichés reveals weakness and confusion: "I am laughing all the way to the poor house. I grinned . . . I just don't know anymore" (31). We know enough about this protagonist and her relationship to her mother to understand why she cannot keep up the original tone of bravado; while she resists her mother with one part of herself, she continues to yearn for her with another part. And we know why she decides to "keep the letter to [herself]" (31): it is a mistake, when dealing with this powerful figure, ever to reveal weakness.

Now having slipped back for a moment into the dangerous world of her mother's power, she tries to return to her safe, dull "holiday." She sees some ants, and then her toes, and their tapping makes her think of a song. Having narcotized herself with these details, she yawns, will perhaps nap, dream, but knows that in a dream the subconscious may once again reassert itself: "I will have a dream, a dream in which I am not sitting on the porch facing the mountains" (32).

In the story's second section Kincaid allows voices from the holiday world to reveal their own emptiness as they speak of their arrangements, their sensibilities, their interesting acquaintances who "know lumber-jacks in Canada" (33). In this world, nature, rather than constituting the visible representation of life's mysteries, is one more product to be critiqued and consumed, previewing the scathing assessment of tourists to come in *A Small Place:* " 'Look at that sunset. Too orange.' 'These pebbles. Not pebbly enough'" (32). Though they are so intent on their own entertainment, these people will later sense how dissatisfying such an existence is; they will look back and be "so pained, so unsettled" (33).

In the next section, as if in retreat from the emptiness of the holiday, the protagonist begins to list all the minor and even laughable things that can go wrong on a holiday, from stinging insects to skunk-perfumed dogs, to fingers sprained playing ball. As is usually the case in Kincaid, however, list making is inspired by a sense of impending loss. Thus, buried in this collection of trivial holiday woes is a vision of death, the "not-too-fast-moving woodchuck" who gets run over, the "prism in the camera broken, because the camera has been exposed in the hot sun" (33). Looking ahead to *Lucy*, we know that the young woman becomes herself a sort of camera, controlling what she sees by turning it into literal and figurative snapshots. And in the final story of *At the Bottom of the River*, Kincaid's protagonist compares herself with a prism, "many-sided and transparent, refracting and reflecting light as it reached me" (80). Here the speaker is a prism reflecting light "that never could be destroyed" (80), and the prism is, as a result, a thing of great beauty. But in "Holidays" the speaker has not managed to come to terms with the powerful light; rather than reflecting its beauty, she is in danger of being destroyed by it. The "sunstroke" (33) that fells the speaker here is only a mild demonstration of the danger the light can cause.

If this powerful light is love, the next section shows again how that light can, by its own intensity, destroy the lens, which would reflect its beauty, for the speaker looks out now and sees a blind man walking by, a man whose love for an unfaithful woman caused him to kill her and, in a suicide attempt, blind himself. Without the light, without vision, the man is a walking death. He speaks to no one and no one speaks to him; even the dogs ignore him. Like the protagonist in the first section, he is alone, walking along the hot road at midday.

In the last two sections of the story, as if frightened by the vision of the man blinded by love, the speaker pulls back. The attempt to rediscover herself has plunged her back into the world she has tried to escape, that of blinding, homicidal love, and so she retreats into a list of holiday highlights, the picturesque sites, the scenery, the laughs. First to be listed are the holiday occupations and pleasures of two boys who "have done many things and taken photographs" (35). Then several dozen impressions from the speaker's own holiday are listed, including such items as "no high heels, buying many funny postcards; sending many funny postcards; taking the rapids; and still, great laughter" (36). If you would escape from yourself, this conclusion seems to say, you must limit yourself to a landscape of disjointed impressions. But, as the opening of the story shows, such disconnectedness produces an agonizing aimlessness, which the mind will always work to escape.

"The Letter from Home," like "Girl," is a three-page-long, one-sentence story. As in "Girl," the story is dominated by a powerful voice, but here we can be less certain about who is speaking. As in the story "At Last," it seems that we are to read the voices of mother and daughter melding into one another. Like "Girl," the story begins with a recounting of the simple and even pleasant details of domestic life: "I milked the cows, I churned the butter, I stored the cheese, I baked the bread, I brewed the tea" (37). Inevitably, this simple, pleasing domestic world begins to shift ominously: "The pot boiled, the gas hissed through the stove, the tree branches heavy with snow crashed against the roof; my heart beat loudly *thud! thud!*, tiny beads of water gathered on my nose, my hair went limp, my waist grew folds, I shed my skin; lips have trembled, tears have flowed, cheeks have puffed, stomachs have twisted with pain" (37).

We know from the story's title that we are dealing with letters from home. These appear frequently in Kincaid's work. In *Lucy*, letters from home are full of grief and warning, telling both of the evils that are likely to befall one who leaves and of the sadness and loss of those who stay behind. The mother's letter responding to Lucy's "very nice" account of a trip on the subway paints such a fearsome picture of what may happen to young girls on a big-city subway that Lucy is "afraid to even put my face outside the door" (20). After this, Lucy saves her mother's letters unopened, including the one telling of her father's death and her mother's destitution.

Letters from home, then, are packets of fear and pain, in which objective accounts quickly veer into visions of destruction. In "The Letter from Home," as in "Girl" and "At Last," one thing always melts into the next; the innocent is always transformed into the frightful. In spite of a kaleidoscopic succession of images, we are in a familiar world, seeing many references that are familiar to Kincaid's readers, such as the woman who sheds her skin as she transforms herself into something else and the ship departing the jetty.

But here a new element appears. Kincaid connects the story of her own world with the great stories of myth and history. If everything changes, do heaven and hell still exist in the way they once did? "Is the Heaven to be above? Is the Hell below? Does the Lamb still lie meek? Does the Lion roar?" And there are the "ancient ships . . . still anchored" (38), ships that may have first brought Europeans or their cargo of slaves to the Caribbean, thus transforming forever the region and the lives of those involved. Even the physical facts of the world are part of a constantly changing story. We know, Kincaid observes, that the earth "spins on its axis" and that "the axis is imaginary" (39).

Kincaid's protagonist has left home, but as we will see again in *Lucy*, home now reaches out to her in the powerfully distilled form of the mother's letters. And what these letters have come to say is that by leaving home one perverts the natural order of things, inviting every kind of tragedy. In "Holidays" the protagonist hides from the consequences of having ripped herself out of the known world, taking refuge in collections of unrelated impressions of her new world. In "The Letter from Home" the act of departure is spun, again and again, into a fabric of chaos and death. At the story's end, the speaker has a direct encounter with death: "I saw a man, He was in a shroud, I sat in a rowboat, He whistled sweetly to me, I narrowed my eyes, He beckoned to me, Come now; I turned and rowed away, as if I didn't know what I was doing" (39).

Here Kincaid's protagonist, as in "Holidays," has found no real defense against the pull of home. In *Lucy* the only defense is to save the letters unopened, to deny knowledge of their well-known content. Here, the protagonist's only defense is to pretend not to understand something she understands all too well.

"What I Have Been Doing Lately" is the last of a trio of stories that seem to reflect the shock and loss of leaving home and the limbo of an as yet unclaimed new world. This story's protagonist goes on a dream journey, circling always back to the point of departure; the journey suggests an endless, vexed cycle in which every leaving is ultimately a return. At the same time, she recognizes that you cannot really go home again, however powerfully you may be drawn back.

In the first lines, the protagonist hears the doorbell ring as she is lying in bed. Perhaps still dreaming, she goes to the door. No one is there, but outside the air is filled with either drizzle or perhaps dust that "tasted like government school ink" (40). Dust-filled air, like the soot that fills the air in Annie John's dream (*AJ*, 112), is used as a signal of change. The soot-filled air signals Annie's collapse. Here the dust, like the suffocating residue of a colonial education, drives the girl away from home and out into the unknown. On this journey, she encounters a great body of water, a barrier familiar in Kincaid's writing. The sea, of course, is prevalent, but a body of water can also be "the tears I had cried," as it is in the story "My Mother," "thick and black and poisonous" with grief (54).

She does not know how to build a bridge across this body of water. She waits. Years pass. Finally, one day "feeling like it, I got into my boat and rowed across" (41). In an unfamiliar land she falls down a deep hole but extricates herself and seems to have gained strength from having passed a significant ordeal. Now she walks on and on, apparently tireless, through a variety of conditions: "I was never thirsty and I felt no pain." Although she is in a world where things and people may look different, she is not threatened: "Looking at the horizon, I made a joke for myself: I said, 'The earth has thin lips,' and I laughed" (42).

Then, as if in response to this moment of ease and confidence, a "lone figure" appears on the horizon, coming toward her. When the figure speaks, it is very much in the style and cadence of the mother we have come to know from "Girl," *Annie John*, and *Lucy*: "'It's you. Just look at that. It's you. And just what have you been doing lately?'" (43). The young woman thinks of several possible replies, one of which subtly defies the mother: "I could have said, 'I have been listening carefully to my mother's words, so as to make a good imitation of a dutiful daughter.'" Instead, however, she is drawn back into the same story again: "I was lying in bed on my back" (43).

At first, the new account appears to be an exact repetition of the one that begins this story. But soon we detect slight changes in language, and then significant changes in the action. In the first account, the speaker looks up, sees the planet Venus, and says, "It must be almost morning" (40). In the second account, she looks up, sees Venus, and says, "If the sun went out, it would be eight minutes before I would know it" (43). Similarly, in the first account, the speaker sees a monkey in a tree and says, "Ah, a monkey. Just look at that monkey" (41). In the second account, she picks up a stone and throws it at the monkey. Three times it moves out of the way; the fourth time the monkey catches the stone and throws it back, striking her and cutting her forehead: "The gash healed immediately but now the skin on my forehead felt false to me" (44). Thus, while the speaker in the first account seems willing simply to notice and accept what she sees around her, in the second story she has become more challenging. Even the sun is no longer what it seems to be. The monkey is now an antagonist, and while the wound it inflicts quickly heals, the evidence of their encounter changes the speaker. She may seem to be caught in an apparently endless cycle of departure and return; nonetheless, her experiences are changing her and the story of self she is able to tell.

When she comes to a body of water, she does not wait for years thinking about a bridge, finally rowing across. Now she simply pays to be ferried across. At this point in the first account, the speaker sees the deep, black hole and willingly falls in. In the second account, she sees some people on a picnic. At first, they seem to be "the most beautiful people" she has ever seen. "Everything about them was black and shiny. Their skin was black and shiny. Their shoes were black and shiny. The clothes they wore were black and shiny." The people are "laughing and chatting" and she goes toward them, but when she gets close she sees them differently: "When I got up close to them I saw that they weren't at a picnic and they weren't beautiful and they weren't chatting and laughing. All around me was black mud and the people all looked as if they had been made up out of black mud" (44). Somehow this new world and the people in it, initially so black and beautiful, has now turned to mud. The sky, which seemed so close in the first account that one could touch it, is now very far away, and feet that never tired from walking earlier now feel "as if they would drop off" (45).

The two accounts differ in a number of ways. In the first, the black-hole experience seems to result in new fortitude; in the second, experiences in the new land bring on exhaustion. In the first account, the figure representing the mother simply appears on the horizon. In the second, the speaker tries to find her or someone like her, tries to get back home. She thinks, "If only just around the bend I would see my house and inside my house I would find my bed, freshly made at that, and in the kitchen I would find my mother or anyone else that I loved making me a custard" (45). But she does not find her house or her mother. She is discouraged in the new world and feels that she cannot go forward. She sees that her experiences are changing her and that she will never be the same as she was before she left. For the moment, the endless story of departure and loss is all she has. Wearily and in great sadness, resting her head on her own knees, she begins the story again, going "back to lying in bed, just before the doorbell rang" (45).

With "Blackness," one of the collection's most powerful pieces, Kincaid begins a new movement, progressing from the denial of loss and the limbo of separation seen in the earlier pieces to a crisis of acceptance. In this, the movement of *At the Bottom of the River* corresponds to that of *Annie John*; the advent of "blackness," like the endless rain in "The Long Rain" chapter, signals not only erasure and silence but also renewal, the possibility of rebirth, and, at the end of both books, the dawning of a new sense of identity, the feel of one's name "filling up" one's mouth (*BR*, 82).

"Blackness" is especially difficult, particularly its first section, one of the most difficult sections in the book. In this story, Kincaid finally escaped the tortured duality that creates the endless cycle of departure and yearning in the previous stories. Here opposites are joined in the concept of "blackness." In Kincaid's "Blackness," Giovanna Covi wrote, "everything is ambiguous, multiple, and fragmented. Blackness is the night that 'falls in silence' as well as the racial color that 'flows through

[the] veins,'" but above all it is what cannot be defined. . . . It is identity together with annihilation of the self" (347).

Annie succumbs to a trancelike state brought on by the rain, is stilled by it, but is also protected by it. So the speaker in this story is "annihilated," "silenced," and "erased" by the blackness (47). At the same time, it is herself: "The blackness cannot be separated from me but often I can stand outside it. . . . The blackness is not my blood, though it flows through my veins" (46). In blackness the self is both completely lost and completely enfolded: "In the blackness my voice is silent . . . then I am swallowed up in the blackness so that I am one with it" (47). Finally, however we read "blackness," whether as general depression or specific grief, what Kincaid seems to convey here is a deeply contradictory vision of identity, a loss of self that is the self. Her aim seems to be, as Covi suggested, to disrupt "binary oppositions" (347) by which life in Western civilization is ordered.

In the second section of the story, a more specific interpretation of "blackness" is possible, one that joins the psychological to the political. Here invading bands of armed men create blackness; they blot out the light, so that "night fell immediately and permanently" (49). In this night the speaker can no longer see flowers, animals, or any of the simple occupations of human life. While the armed men are not identified, this passage is similar to one found in Kincaid's story "Ovando." Here Ovando, a European conqueror in the Caribbean, has a similar effect on the landscape. For no particular reason, other than celebration of his "Sheer Might," Ovando lays waste the world of the story's speaker, doing so in such a way that even the light of the sun is blotted out (79).

In "Ovando," Kincaid elaborated on the multifarious nature of "night" in a way which is not only reminiscent of a story discussed earlier, "In the Night," but which may also help us to understand the ambiguity of "Blackness." Ovando the conqueror, who has caused darkness to fall on the land,

> lived constantly in night; but it was not a quiet night, a night that bore a soft sleep in which dreams of a long-ago-lived enchanted childhood occurred; it was not the sort of night that the day angrily interrupts, jealous of the union between the sleeper and the borderless, soft tapestry of blackness; and it was not a night of nature, which is to say the progression from the day to the opposite of day; it was not the night of just after sunset or the night of just before the sun rises. Ovando lived in the thickest part of the night, the deepest part of the night, the part of the night where all suffering dwells, including death; the part of the night in

which the weight of the world is made visible and eternal terror is confirmed. (82)

In both "Ovando" and the second section of "Blackness," we see how
varied blackness or darkness may be. It may be as welcome as the
embrace of a lover, or it may be the seat of suffering and the confirmation of terror. It may be part of the natural cycle of renewal, or it may be
a blight caused by those who appear to be empty of all but a will to
power.

In the third section of "Blackness," a mother describes a daughter.
The voice, however, is not the voice of the mother we have come to
know. This speaker focuses intently on the daughter in a way that the
mother of "Girl," for example, with her constant attacks and reversals, is
never capable of doing. This speaker, while seeing a daughter from a
mother's point of view, closely resembles the daughter-protagonist. In
response to "blackness"—the loss of self that paradoxically is the self—
Kincaid invented a mother who will allow identity to develop. While the
mother in "Girl" seeks to trap her daughter between a litany of requirements and the certainty that the girl can never live up to these requirements, the mother fashioned here, another of Kincaid's othermothers,
neither molds nor chastises, but grasps and celebrates, both the immense
energy and the unfettered, contradictory nature of the daughter, this
spirit that she has "summoned . . . into a fleeting existence" (51).

Through the eyes of this othermother, the girl not only embraces contradictions but is herself a physical contradiction, both child and mon-
ster. In this, oddly, the girl has been granted a kind of personhood
previously denied. Formerly, it has been the adult women, particularly
the mother, who had possessed the power of such transformation—the
woman who "removed her skin" and became a bird, for example, and
the jablesse who masquerades as a beautiful woman, both in "The
Night." Here, for the first time, Kincaid's young protagonist is granted
this power, and what is more important, she is granted it by the all-powerful mother, who sees and reports the transformation.

In the story's last section, blackness is replaced by "the silent voice,"
which the speaker "moves toward" in love and which so completely
"enfolds" her "that even in memory the blackness is erased" (52). Still,
the silence and blackness are similar. The speaker is "at peace" in the
silent voice but also, as in blackness, "erased."

One way to consider this enigmatic section may be to compare it to
the "Long Rain" section of *Annie John*. The sickness engulfing Annie is

also a kind of blackness that has seemed to fill the air with soot (112). This condition ceases at the same moment that the long rain suddenly ceases. The sound of the rain pounding on the roof "pressed [Annie] down in [her] bed, bolted [her] down." But at the end of the sickness, the rain and the sound of its incessant pounding stop.

In *Annie John*, then, silence replaces blackness after Annie's figurative rebirthing by her grandmother replaces the bitter relationship that has grown up between Annie and her mother. Awakening from her illness, Annie is not content with the world she finds herself in, but no longer paralyzed, she is beginning down the road toward self-fashioning. In "Blackness" the "silent voice" replaces "blackness" after the protagonist has been, in a sense, remothered; the maternal voice of "Girl," with her impossible-to-meet standards, has been replaced by a mother who applauds the vast, contradictory nature of the child's spirit. Perhaps, then, the final section of "Blackness" presents the moment in which the oppressiveness of control is replaced by the void of sudden freedom. The protagonist is no longer herself as she has known herself ("I am no longer 'I'" [52]), for she has been, in blackness, erased. And while the act of erasure can be interpreted as a murder of the self, it can also be read as the opposite, a necessary emptying out that signals the birth of identity.

As she battles toward a separate identity, Kincaid's daughter figure is no longer the inarticulate, nearly paralyzed receptor of her mother's will and power, as in "Girl." The daughter in "My Mother" has become the mother's open, if ambivalent, antagonist, and the two are caught, as the story's first section shows, in a mutually murderous embrace. The daughter wishes the mother dead, immediately repents and is forgiven, and is taken into the mother's arms, where she is held "closer and closer to her bosom, until finally I suffocated" (53). Even in apparent reconciliation there is bitterness; the tears the daughter has cried now form a pond that is "thick and black and poisonous" (54), across which mother and daughter eye each other. Not only are they separated, apparently permanently, by a grief that cannot be dissipated, but as if to signal the depth of their separation, they have each begun falsely to "shower the other with words and deeds of love and affection" (54).

In the story's second section, the mother appears to engage the daughter in an obeah ceremony. While the daughter sits on her mother's bed, the mother darkens the room, blocking the entrance of any outside light, and then lights candles, causing the shadows of the two figures to take on a life of their own. The shadows make "a place between themselves, as if they were making room for someone else" (54), but nothing comes to fill the space. We remember here that in *Annie John* and "Antigua Crossing," the mother believes the daughter is the object of an obeah spell worked by women who once loved the girl's father. In *Annie John* a spell is suspected as the cause of Annie's illness, while in the earlier piece, "Antigua Crossing," spells are suspected of having caused the girl's "overly troublesomeness," resulting in the girl being sent from Antigua to her maternal grandmother on the nearby island of Dominica. In this context, the obeah ceremony comes to represent the mother's attempt to address the difficulty existing between her daughter and herself, to discover what it is that has come between them, as she watches to see what will fill up the space between their two shadows.

If the mother seeks to understand their estrangement as an evil spell, however, and to discover the author of that spell, she fails. Nothing comes to fill the space between the two shadows, and even the magical light of the obeah candles seems to fail as the shadows in the room take on the complexity of shadows "controlled by the light of day" (54). The mother finally blows out the candles; the shadows vanish. The daughter, still sitting on the bed, tries "to get a good look at [herself]" (55). The mother obscures both the girl's and her own ability to study what is really happening, insisting on there being a magical cause for the estrangement.

In the third section of the story, we see the mother again involved in magic, finally caught in the act of transformation that has been hinted at throughout these stories. Here, with the calm and practiced gestures of a woman at her toilette, she removes her clothes and her hair, grows scales, flattens her eyes on top of her head, where they spin and blaze. Throughout the ceremony of this story's previous section, the daughter remains herself. But now the mother's power is overwhelming. In the face of this transformative ability, the girl obeys the instruction to "follow [her mother's] example," and she, too, becomes a serpent. Now she, too, "travel[s] along on [her] white underbelly, [her] tongue darting and flickering in the hot air." The daughter is still dominated by the mother; at the same time, she demonstrates that she is coming into the dangerous power of a full-grown woman.

In the fourth section, the daughter, though still overpowered by the mother, has grown to titanic proportions. Her mother is still bigger and stronger than she; nevertheless, the daughter feels herself expanding, understanding that she has so perfectly learned the art of manipulation from her mother that she is able to use it against her mother. As the daughter senses her own growing powers, she guards herself by pretending weakness. In the battle of manipulation, love and pity are prime

weapons: "To make sure she believed in my frailness, I sighed occasionally—long soft sighs, the kind of sigh she had long ago taught me could
evoke sympathy" (55–56). In spite of the changes occurring in the
daughter, mother and daughter are still linked together, and in this con-
figuration, the mother will always be more powerful, able to reduce the
daughter into childishness: "I let out a horrible roar, then a self-pitying
whine. I had grown big, but my mother was bigger, and that would
always be so" (56).

In the story's fifth section, mother and daughter enter a dark, cold
cave. The daughter remains there for years, adapting to the dark and
cold conditions, growing a "special lens" that allows her to see and a
"special coat" with which to keep warm (57). Whether we read the cave
as simply the loss of the mother's love, or more literally as a new, cold
world—such as the New York of *Lucy*, to which the protagonist must
flee—it is clear that the mother mocks the daughter's effort to adapt,
remarking on the "strange expression you have on your face. So cross, so
miserable, as if you were living in a climate not suited to your nature"
(57). Again, we are reminded of *Lucy*, where the mother, in response to
a "nice letter" from her daughter telling of her first subway ride, writes
back to detail the hideous crimes she has read about that have been committed against immigrant girls in the subway (20).

Increasingly willing to fight back, the daughter tries to trap the
mother, building a beautiful house over a deep hole and then inviting
the mother inside, "hoping to hear her land with a thud at the bottom"
(57). But the daughter is not yet the match of a mother who has vast
experience in expecting things not to be what they seem. The mother
does not fall to the bottom of the hole, but walks on the air as if it were
the most solid of floors.

In the story's fifth and sixth sections, the daughter realizes that
despite her own growing power, her mother will always be more powerful and that this power will always be used to dominate her. In the
story's seventh section, the girl sets off on a sea voyage reminiscent of
the end of *Annie John*, leaving the mother for the first time. But while
Annie John ends at this point, "My Mother" carries the girl through the
voyage, depositing her on an island where she is greeted by a woman
whose "face was completely different from what I was used to" but
whom the girl still recognizes as her mother: "We greeted each other at
first with great caution and politeness, but as we walked along, our steps
became one, and as we talked, our voices became one voice, and we were
in complete union in every other way. What peace came over me then,

for I could not see where she left off and I began, or where I left off and
she began" (59–60).

Initially, we seem to have entered another of the endless cycles of
departure from and return to the mother, similar to that in "A Letter
from Home." But when "My Mother" is considered against both
"Antigua Crossings" and *Annie John*, it appears that something significantly different is happening. We notice first that the "mother" who
greets the narrator after her voyage and takes her home is no longer
mocking and that her embrace is no longer murderous. Rather, mother
and daughter come together with blissful ease: "I fit perfectly in the
crook of my mother's arm, on the curve of her back, in the hollow of her
stomach" (60). Their union is similar to the rebirthing of Annie John by
her grandmother, Ma Chess. Annie says, "I would lie on my side, curled
up like a little comma, and Ma Chess would lie next to me, curled up
like a bigger comma, into which I fit" (*AJ*, 126).

In "Antigua Crossing" there is another depiction of a young woman
who leaves her troubled relationship with her mother and voyages to her
grandmother. When the girl arrives, she immediately recognizes her
grandmother and feels she would have done so even if she had never seen
a photograph. The grandmother immediately begins to work her protective magic, walking the girl to the water and making her "spit in the
sea three times" (50).

The voyage in "My Mother," then, seems to be away from the mother we have known up to now and toward the othermother who steps in
to nurture the girl when her own mother fails to meet her needs.
Kincaid herself made such a journey to escape an obeah spell (Simmons),
and there may be a literal, autobiographical basis for the fictional journey from mother to grandmother. This story, like *Annie John* and
"Antigua Crossing," nonetheless requires us to see the journey as an act
of spiritual faith. The voyage does not merely replace one mother with
another but also works to break an evil spell. The rupture between
mother and daughter is seen not as a problem of personalities but as evidence of something amiss in the world as the result of malignant inter-
vention. In all three works, the spell is finally broken by the voyage to
the magical othermother.

In the world of the new "mother" all is harmonious, and we sense a
quiet anticipation, as if the narrator is waiting to be reborn into a happi-
er life. Whereas a house is the scene of murderous combat between
mother and daughter in the last section, here a house is a continuous
procession of spacious rooms to be filled with new life. Mother and

daughter walk though rooms that are "large and empty, opening on to each other, waiting for people and things to fill them up" (60). Again, as if awaiting a birth or rebirth, the two are described in terms that imply the simultaneous union and separateness of mother and unborn child: "We merge and separate, merge and separate; soon we shall enter the final stage of our evolution" (60).

In this story, the girl has fully recognized her mother as her antagonist and, having exhausted herself trying to combat the mother, has fled, crossing the water, breaking the spell, finding on the other side another mother figure who nurses her back to life. Whether this other-mother represents an actual autobiographical grandmother or an imaginary figure growing out of the narrator's intense desire for nurturance and a world that is friendly and reliable rather than ever-devious and changing, her presence begins a new movement in the story. The narrator is still unformed, an infant "sitting on my mother's enormous lap" (61). But the two dwell in a world that is welcoming, arranging itself for them in obedience to the mother's benevolent magic: "The fishermen are coming in from the sea; their catch is bountiful, my mother has seen to that" (60). While nature has been seen as treacherously impermanent in earlier stories, here it can be trusted; here the two "live in a bower made from flowers whose petals are imperishable" (61). And while earlier fantasies of union with the mother, such as that at the end of "In the Night," represent an impossible return to a lost past, this vision is concerned not with the past but the future. The narrator in the earlier stories is always the child in relation to the mother, impending maturity seen as a crime. Here, however, though the narrator is seen as an infant, she also contains the seeds of her own healthy maturity: "A hummingbird has nested on my stomach, a sign of my fertileness" (61).

With the collection's final story, Kincaid completes the emotional journey begun with "Girl." Her narrator has accepted the loss of a childhood sense of love and perfection and, with great difficulty, has managed to replace the lost beauty with a more mature vision of her place in creation. If Kincaid's protagonist has still lost a paradise, she has also gained a self. The tongue-tied girl of "Girl," mesmerized by her mother's voice, is transformed into the world-striding woman in the final story; she now owns and belongs to a beautiful, impartial, albeit transient creation, her own name finally "filling up" (82) her mouth.

While "At the Bottom of the River" completes this journey, the story shows the link between the loss of childhood paradise and the perception of death, which was only peripherally apparent earlier. Here, at last, the protagonist has stopped clinging to her childhood and has survived the shock of the immediate loss. But maturity implies the inevitability of death, and we come to see that the protagonist, in resisting maturity, has also been resisting death. Further, the mother's denial of the child's innocence and love amounts to a kind of death sentence. That connection is made in this story as a "you," speaking in a voice that we recognize as the mother's, laughingly announces the girl's death:"'Death is natural,' you said to me, in such a flat, matter-of-fact way, and then you laughed—a laugh so piercing that I felt my eardrums shred, I felt myself mocked"(71).

How can this new terrain, in which death is a sudden and overpowering presence, be understood? What is the meaning of an existence that, like a deep stream, rushes forward with great force and energy and then "collects itself in a pool" at the end of day (63)?

Having asked this question, Kincaid seems to examine, and then to dismiss, two ways of finding "meaning." One way is that of a man who, like the European conqueror and title character of the story "Ovando," is dead to the beautiful, contradictory energy of life and who "sits in nothing, this man: not in a full space not in emptiness, not in darkness, not in light or glimmer of. He sits in nothing, in nothing, in nothing" (BR, 64). The second way is embodied in another man whom Kincaid dismisses, if more gently, this one resembling the carpenter father described in Annie John and, more particularly, the father in one of her New Yorker pieces, a calm, precise man in a brown felt hat.[1] This man is not dead to the world around him; rather, he is very much alive to its beauty and mystery. But for him, too, it all comes to nothing, and death still looms so prominently as to negate experience: "Stretching out before him is a silence so dreadful, a vastness, its length and breadth and depth immeasurable. Nothing" (BR, 68). For both the conqueror, who tries to control life, and the conquered, who simply gazes at it in blank wonder, the result is the same, a dreadful emptiness.

Then, in the story's long third section, the narrator seems to give herself up to grief, as she laments the bitter inevitability and ubiquity of death: "Dead is the past. Dead shall the future be. And what stands before my eyes, as soon as I turn my back, dead is that, too" (69). It is here that the mother, with a laugh, declares that "death is natural," but the narrator protests that death "bears no relation to the tree, the sea, the twittering bird. How much more like the earth spinning on its invisible axis death is" (72). Death, then, seems unrelated to the natural drive of nature, but appears instead as some awful abstraction.

In the story's fourth section, the narrator takes one last look at the lost paradise of childhood, in which death was unknown: "Time and again, I am filled up with all that I thought life might be—glorious moment upon glorious moment of contentment and joy and love running into each other and forming an extraordinary chain: a hymn sung in rounds" (74). But after lingering for a moment the narrator tears herself away, turning back to the pool of deep water that now represents life and the mysteries of maturity.

The book's final movement now begins. Kincaid's protagonist looks into the water and sees a house. Previously, houses have appeared as the sites of mutual manipulation by mother and daughter or of the narrator's return to the womb (both in "My Mother"). Here, at last, she sees a grown woman in the house, a woman of vision, and a woman who is, finally, herself. What the woman sees and leads the narrator to see is a world in which things are themselves, in which they cannot be changed when a new light is cast upon them. When light falls on a thing, it seems "transparent, as if the light went through each thing, so that nothing could be hidden. The light shone and shone and fell and fell, but there were no shadows. . . . And in this world were many things blessed with unquestionable truth and purpose and beauty" (77–78).

In a world in which things are themselves, it suddenly becomes possible that one may be oneself, may see oneself in a way that cannot be changed by the view of another, and here the narrator for the first time sees herself clearly, as if "looking through a plane of glass," describing herself in loving detail (79).

Fully herself at last, she enters the sea, "warm as freshly spilled blood" (79), and is then "dipped again and again, over and over, in a large vat filled with precious elements" (80). After these two baths—resembling both the amniotic fluid of the womb and the obeah bath with which Ma Chess ritually reconnects herself to nature—-the protagonist stands "as if I were a prism, many-sided and transparent, refracting and reflecting light as it reached me, light that never could be destroyed. And how beautiful I became" (80).

"Yet," Kincaid's narrator finally asks, "what was this light?" What illumination may be embraced "until heart and glowing thing are indistinguishable and in this way the darkness is made less?" (81). For Kincaid, the secret of the light seems to be that it comes not from any controlling force but from a creation that is "impartial" and "whose nature is implacable, unmindful of any of the individual needs of existence, and without knowledge of future or past" (81).

In the beginning of *At the Bottom of the River*, Kincaid's protagonist struggles with the sense that the perfection of childhood can be replaced only by forces of manipulation and control, and so she clings to a lost perfection. Ultimately worn out by this hopeless effort, she allows herself to be born into maturity. Now she is able to see that while childhood and one's own innocence and sense of timelessness may be lost, these qualities still exist in creation. In this clear light, different from the shadowy light of manipulation, she is able to see herself and able to accept her place in creation, understanding "how bound up I know I am to all that is human endeavor, to all that is past and to all that shall be, to all that shall be lost and leave no trace" (82).

Chapter Seven

Annie John: Coming of Age in the West Indies

With *Annie John*, Jamaica Kincaid's writing became greatly more accessible than in *At the Bottom of the River*. Here, as her own book jacket could proclaim, was "the traditional story of a young girl's passage into adolescence," but one that "pulsates with the exotic rhythms of the islands." *Annie John* was widely and favorably reviewed by critics, who no longer complained of difficulty in grasping what was behind Kincaid's beautiful language. Rather, they found the book "touching and familiar" (Kenney, 6), animated by "the power to bring home emotion so simply and directly."[1] Reviewers noted that Kincaid covers "almost the same ground" as in *At the Bottom of the River* but that her "fractured descriptions" have given way to a story that is "episodic" and more obviously "autobiographical."[2]

Yet *Annie John*'s apparent simplicity is deceptive. Behind the book's picturesque scenes of uniformed colonial schoolgirls and graceful West Indian women in big, brightly colored skirts, behind the stories of schoolgirl crushes and first menstruation, looms an overpowering specter of betrayal and death. As in J. D. Salinger's coming-of-age classic *Catcher in the Rye*, impending maturity and the sexuality that inevitably accompanies it are seen as deadly enemies of childhood's beauty and purity.

Like Salinger's Holden Caulfield, Annie John clings to the world of childhood innocence that is slipping away and gazes obsessively at the degradation that seems to replace it. But while Kincaid's book bears many similarities to Salinger's, the two books also have important differences, reflecting differing cultural visions of maturity itself.

In Salinger's book a well-honed sense of hypocrisy, the "phoniness" so apparent to Holden, allows adults to hold in safe solution the yearnings and perceptions of the individual spirit and the compromises one must make to pursue success and status. This hypocritical maturity is commended by all—parents, teachers, even young friends—and is there for Holden to embrace if and when he is willing to do so. Holden has the luxury of choosing to reject the adult world. The adult world does not reject him or castigate him for his own incipient maturity; rather, it waits confidently for him to take his place among the other smooth and successful "phonies," that is, the adults.

In Annie's world, however, as defined by her all-powerful mother, there is no viable maturity. Furthermore, the girl's involuntary onset of maturation is treated by the mother as a kind of crime for which she must be punished. While Holden resists the readily apparent route of successful maturation by flunking out of one school after another, Annie tries to find a way to mature acceptably, hoping to win back her mother's affection by excelling in her studies. Yet, for Annie, unlike Holden, there appears to be no route to successful maturation; indeed, there can be no such thing, for order in her mother's kingdom—and by reflection in colonial Antigua—requires more than a willingness to submerge the individual point of view in the societal soup. What Annie's mother knows, if only subconsciously, is that any authentic individual point of view held by black Antiguans would be so thoroughly antithetical to the British values and ideals by which colonial society is ordered that the two cannot be allowed to coexist. To the black islanders, successful maturity requires not that the individual point of view be submerged, as in Holden Caulfield's world, but that one not have an individual point of view at all or rather that the black Antiguans' point of view *be* the British point of view. The colonial schoolchildren are not taught the art of civilized hypocrisy, as in Holden's world, but rather to "proudly [witness] against themselves from a British perspective."[3] For the colonial child of African descent, maturity, with its awareness of individuality, is by definition a kind of crime against the social order, one that must be punished. Individuality must die as schoolchildren internalize—learn "by heart" (Tiffin, 32)—the literature and thus the cultural assumptions of the British Empire.

Holden Caulfield's struggle to mature brings on a breakdown, and he addresses his readers from some sort of institution in California where he has gone to "take it easy."[4] He does not know whether he will begin applying himself in school or not when he gets out, but he is planning to drive home in his brother D.B.'s Jaguar, paid for by D.B.'s "prostitut[ion]" in the film business (Salinger, 2). Holden can join if he wants; if he declines to join, it is by choice. But in Annie's world there is no such volition. She cannot truly join the world of maturity or decline to join, since she will never have what it takes to be a fully enfranchised adult; she will never be white and British. Thus, while Holden emerges from his breakdown still debating whether he will "apply himself" in school, Annie emerges from her breakdown with the clear sense that she must leave the world as she knows it to save her sanity and her soul.

It is not surprising that Kincaid's coming-of-age novel, taking place in a world where a black girl's maturation inaugurates a lifelong struggle to avoid the death of the spirit, begins with an obsession with death, and particularly the death of little girls. What may seem surprising is that Annie does not see death coming to her at the hands of the colonial government; rather, she associates death with her mother, who is often accidentally present when someone dies, who bathes the dead, and who seems to carry death about on her hands. The mother has not exactly suffered spiritual death herself, but when it comes to coping with her daughter's burgeoning maturity, she seems to have internalized the "'half devil,' 'half child'" (Tiffin, 32) characterization of colonized peoples inculcated by the ruling power. It follows that if Annie is no longer part child, she must be all devil. The mother who has previously been able to see her daughter as all child, with all the innocent perfection of any child, now sees the same girl as a liar, a thief, and a "slut" who must be expelled from the "paradise" of mother's love into the living death of a loveless purgatory.

For a time, Annie fights against this new development, first trying to win back her mother's love and then trying to replace it with attachments to other girls. Along with them, she tries to hold off the future and the spiritual death that all seem to sense will accompany it. With her school friends Annie feels temporarily safe, and buoyed by the "powerful feeling" she has in their still-innocent and vigorous company, Annie glancingly acknowledges the role of the white "masters" in defining her future: "What perfection we found in each other," she says, "sitting on these tombstones of long dead people who had been the masters of our ancestors! . . . We were sure that the much-talked-about future that everybody was preparing us for would never come, for we had such a powerful feeling against it, and why shouldn't our will prevail this time?" (50). But the triumph over the white masters is illusory. Adolescence progresses, and with it the devastation of the secure and welcoming world Annie had known as a child.

It is the universal condition that adolescence both disrupts the certainties of childhood and challenges the compromises of adulthood. But Kincaid's *Annie John*, along with other coming-of-age novels by West Indian women born in the 1940s, suggests that, for this generation at least, childhood is particularly prized and, correspondingly, the onset of maturity is particularly difficult to negotiate. In Erna Brodber's *Jane and Louisa Will Soon Come Home*, set in Jamaica, the girl Nellie's "Edenic" existence is destroyed as maturity "brings with it a series of exposures and revelations that shatter Nellie's sense of herself. She becomes aware of color and class divisions in her family and her community, recognizes the 'shame' and 'filth' and precariousness of being female. . . . It adds up to more than our heroine can bear and she suffers total psychic collapse."[5] For Nellie, as for Annie John, the onset of puberty is shameful, a kind of crime that changes others' attitudes toward the girl:

> My mother, in her dead-pan voice that I cannot figure calls out to me. It is not her scolding voice, it is not her praising voice. So what is it. No eye contact and she is pretending to sew. My God. I'm hardly eleven. What shame have you to hide from me?
> Silence
> —You are eleven now and soon something strange will happen to you—
> Silence; still no eye contact.
> —Well, when it does, make sure you tell your aunt—
> Period. End of sentence. I presume I am dismissed. Finished. Best to forget all this strangeness but Lord, it's eating up the world.[6]

In Merle Hodge's novel *Crick Crack, Monkey*, set in Trinidad, it is not burgeoning sexuality that destroys the Eden of childhood but the opportunity for formal education. When young Tee wins a prestigious secondary school scholarship, she must be torn from her loving, self-knowing, earthy aunt Tantie and taken to live with her anxious, striving-to-be-white Aunt Beatrice. Like the mother of Kincaid's infancy, Tantie loves herself and the child; both feel at home in their skins. But like the mother of Kincaid's adolescence, Aunt Beatrice seems to know neither herself nor the child. She, along with the school authorities, assesses value in terms of "lightness" and of one's ability to emulate the British. Anathema for her is not "sluttishness" but "niggeryness." Tee, unappreciated and ignored, even though she excels in her studies, is suddenly fawned upon by students and teacher alike when it is learned that she will be leaving the island to join her father in England.

The conflicting values of youth and maturity in the West Indies result in collapse for Kincaid's and Hodge's protagonists, whereas in *Crick Crack, Monkey*, Tee mediates the conflict by inventing a double, Helen, an English girl of her age and height, who does English things like visit her grandmother to sit "by the fireside" having "tea with delicious scones and home-made strawberry jam."[7] So powerful, so right in the world is Helen, that once conceived, she seems to be more than a double. Indeed, she seems to be "the Proper Me. And me, I was her shadow hovering about in incompleteness" (Hodge, 62).

At the end of both Kincaid's and Hodge's novels, the young protagonists must reject both the beloved mother of infancy and the despised mother of adolescence. Each girl sees departure for England not as a triumph or an opportunity but a relief. At the same time, both leave with a sense of great loss. For Tee, everything in her childhood home is "unrecognizable, pushing me out" (Hodge, 110). For Annie, the sensation of leaving also resembles an "emptying out" (*AJ*, 148).

Both Kincaid and Hodge write of a lost paradise, and the assault on the spirit and identity that comes with a West Indian adolescence. Both reject the mother figures who first introduce them to paradise and then seem to snatch it from them. At the same time, both writers find a source of hope and strength as they set out to build an identity that is neither "child" nor "devil." This source is, for both Annie and Tee, a magical grandmother figure, one who inhabits a still-enchanted world. As Helen Pyne Timothy suggested of Annie's Ma Chess, both grandmothers seem to belong to an "older generation of Caribbean women" for whom "the penetration of European cultural values in the African cosmology was not so intense or so desirable" (242).

In Hodge's book, Tee's grandmother, Ma, who lives up in the hills, seems to inhabit "an enchanted country" that calls up fantasies of "the days when Brar Anancy and Brar Leopard and all the others roamed the earth outsmarting each other" (14). Ma dies at the end of the book, and on the surface, this seems to be another loss for Tee to bear. Much earlier, however, the grandmother has offered an identity to the girl that, despite her sorrow, she seems to be "growing into," for the grandmother sees in the girl the spirit of her own grandmother: "She couldn't remember her grandmother's true-true name. But Tee was growing into her grandmother again, her spirit was in me. They'd never bent down her spirit and she would come back and come back and come back" (19).

Similarly, Ma Chess, who is still in touch with the ancient spirits, cures Annie of her mysterious illness through a symbolic rebirthing. Reborn, Annie still feels the loss of her childhood happiness but is no longer paralyzed by this loss, and so she is able to set about finding her own identity and name.

Death is not unknown to the young protagonist of *Annie John*; in this world, the dead are likely to reappear, to wait for you under a tree, or even to follow you home. But, while Annie has shivered at the idea of the dead reappearing, she has never worried about dying, since she assumes this is something that happens to adults she does not know. In the book's first chapter, however, the realization that children can die appears literally on the horizon of the ten-year-old girl's life in the form of "small, sticklike figures" the girl sees "bobbing up and down in the distance" (4) as funeral processions pass. The processions that take place in the evening are for the funerals of adults, Annie's mother tells her, but those in the morning are usually for the funerals of children. "Until then," Annie says, "I had not known that children died" (4). Then death moves in even closer. A girl named Nalda dies and then a "humpback" girl of Annie's own age. And adults to whom Annie has a connection die—first, the mother of another little girl, Sonia, and then a neighbor, Miss Charlotte.

In all these deaths there are patterns. First, the little girls who die or are associated with death are badly cared for and somehow deformed or peculiar. Nalda "liked to eat mud" and was dressed in a very "unbecoming" way by her mother (5). The humpback girl, besides her deformity, had badly combed hair, and looking at the crooked part one day when the girl was still alive, Annie sees that she "must have combed her hair herself" (10). Sonia, the girl whose mother died, is a "dunce" whom Annie loves to pet and torment. The death of Sonia's mother is seen as abandonment; afterward, Annie never speaks to the girl again: "She seemed such a shameful thing, a girl whose mother had died and left her alone in the world" (8).

A second pattern emerges in the deaths Annie observes; her own mother often seems to have an intimate association with the death or the dead person. On several occasions, the mother is on hand when someone dies. The girl Nalda dies in Annie's mother's arms, and the neighbor, Miss Charlotte, "collapsed and died while having a conversation with [Annie's] mother," who catches the dead woman as she falls to the ground (8). Annie's mother prepares Nalda for burial and now seems to carry death on her hands: "For a while, though not for very long, I could not bear to have my mother caress me or touch my food or help me with my bath. I especially couldn't bear the sight of her hands lying still in her lap" (6).

Death, then, is seen here as something that happens to deformed or improperly nurtured children; further, Annie's own mother seems to be on strangely intimate terms with death, a kind of priestess of death. Seen in this light, death is not just a random act of fate but a kind of betrayal and abandonment peculiarly related to mother love. Thus, even before any overt break between Annie and her mother occurs, even when Annie is still the object of her mother's doting attention, the girl seems to glimpse fearfully a connection between her mother's nurturing capacities and the death of children, a connection that will soon be transformed into one between the mother and the death of childhood.

The dislocations of puberty have not yet occurred in this chapter; nonetheless, they are signaled when Annie's obsession with death leads to the first reported rift between mother and daughter. A voyeuristic visit to the funeral of the humpback girl causes Annie to get home late, to forget an important errand, and to attempt to cover up the omission with a lie, for which she is punished. Though no physical maturation has begun, Annie's maturing mind struggles with a changed perception of reality, and this, inevitably it seems, leads her into crime.

In the book's second chapter, Kincaid describes the "paradise" of her childhood and shows how this paradise is created by the mother. We see again the instructing mother of "Girl," with her litany of household advice, but here we see an added dimension in the beauty the girl finds in her mother's daily activities and the child's joy at being allowed to spend "the day following my mother around and observing the way she did everything" (15).

The world belongs to the mother and so, very much, does the child, whose life is symbolically contained within her mother's life, just as the mementos of her childhood are contained within her mother's trunk. The mother arranges and caresses the items in the trunk, telling stories, as she does so, of the girl's infancy. The sessions with the trunk are for the child a feast of love as she sits next to her mother, smelling her fragrance, watching her lips move as she speaks. Annie is conscious of how happy she is in her mother's love: "It was in such a paradise that I lived" (25).

But with puberty this paradise is lost. Annie turns 12, grows tall, develops a different smell, and suddenly is no longer welcome in her mother's world. The mother harshly decrees that they can no longer dress identically and no longer have time to browse through the trunk of childhood memorabilia. Rather than spend her days following her mother about, Annie is now sent for various sorts of lessons intended to make her a "young lady."

Returning home from Sunday school with a prize for Bible study, Annie hopes to "reconquer" her mother; instead, she walks in upon her

parents making love and is transfixed by the sight of her mother's hand:
"It was white and bony, as if it had long been dead and had been left out
in the elements. . . . If I were to forget everything else in the world, I
could not forget her hand as it looked then. I could also make out that
the sounds I had heard were her kissing my father's ears and his mouth
and his face. I looked at them for I don't know how long" (30–31). And
Annie is sure that she can never let the hand touch her again or let her
mother kiss her again.

In the first chapter, death appears as a mysterious phenomenon,
unexplained, yet somehow connected to flawed or ill-cared-for children,
and to Annie's mother. Here another mystery appears: puberty and the
maternal rejection that has accompanied it are somehow connected to
sex and to death. The mother, who has controlled the world, must control these new elements too. Indistinctly, the mother is seen as hideously
duplicitous, both rejecting the daughter as a result of her imminent
maturity and engaging in the activity that is most obviously associated
with this killing maturity.

In the first of several attempts to replace her mother's love, Annie
falls in love with one of her classmates, a girl named Gwen. And, at a
new school, Annie distinguishes herself among her classmates by writing
an acclaimed essay, making herself the adored center of the school world
as she has been the adored center of her mother's world.

With the essay, Annie seeks to establish her identity outside her
mother's circle of power, but must do so in terms of the central conflict
of her life, the maternal rift. The essay describes Annie and her mother
taking a medicinal bath in the sea, swimming naked like two "sea mammals" (42). This blissful, amniotic moment, in which "all the sounds" of
the sea seem to be coming from inside the mother, is disrupted by "three
ships going by" (43). Loud celebrations are taking place on the ships;
they are cruise ships, bringing tourists to the Caribbean, though perhaps
they also represent the three ships of Columbus's voyage. Their arrival
disrupts the blissful scene, and in panic, Annie realizes she has lost sight
of her mother. Behind the mother's desertion, Kincaid seems to say, is an
invasion that destroys the harmonies of their world.

As the essay goes on, the girl glimpses her mother sitting on a rock a
small distance away but cannot reach her and cries herself into exhaustion. When the mother returns, she comforts the girl and tells her she
will never leave her. Later, Annie dreams of the incident, but the mother
again comforts and reassures her. The essay is true, Annie reports, except

for the ending. In fact, the mother turned her back on the girl when told of the bad dreams and warned her about eating unripe fruit.

With this story, which is reminiscent of the scenarios described in *At the Bottom of the River*—the bliss of the amniotic bath, then the girl and her mother divided by a body of salt water, both sea and tears—Annie begins to struggle with the question of her new identity. Who is she if not the infant, blissfully encircled by its mother, defined by protection and love? The real situation with her mother has provided no answer, and so Annie has invented a story—similar to the fantasies of union in *At the Bottom of the River*—in which the separation has occurred and the grief has been felt, but in the end, the mother's love proves sustaining.

The essay is the object of "adoration" by Annie's new schoolmates and causes Gwen to "fall in love" with her. The reason the essay so moves the girls is not explicitly given, but as Annie reports their conversations later in the chapter, all of the girls seem to dread the future that "everybody was preparing us for" (50); thus, Annie's essay may have spoken to a generally felt fear that what has sustained the girls in childhood will be ripped from them as they enter maturity. Though Annie's story ends with a lie, it speaks comfortingly to the girl's own fears, and as a result, the story's author is an instant heroine.

Annie has succeeded temporarily in recreating a new world to replace the one that has been lost. Once again, she is at the center of an adoring universe. As she seeks to replace her mother's affection with that of her schoolmates, she focuses on one particular girl, Gwen. Now, Annie tells Gwen, it will not matter so much if the mother dies; now it is Gwen and Annie who will live together forever in the same house, not Annie and her mother.

But this attempt to dissipate the grief of impending maturity through schoolgirl love and solidarity is doomed to failure. Soon Annie begins to menstruate, and while the other girls are excited and envious, all sense that something tragic has happened, demonstrating that their love for one another cannot save them from maturity and thus from a "future full of ridiculous demands." It is as if someone or something has died, and after Annie's revelation the girls "walked back to class slowly, as if going to a funeral." Annie and Gwen vow that their love will continue, but the unquestionable fact of approaching maturity has already separated them, and their words "had a hollow ring and when we looked at each other we couldn't sustain the gaze" (53).

After failing to replicate the universe of maternal love with Gwen and her school friends, Annie now grows more rebellious as she takes up with the unwashed, unfettered Red Girl, who is everything Annie's mother disapproves of. Annie had formerly thought her own world a "paradise"; she now finds perfection in the Red Girl's careless ways, her refusal to wash or live in a ladylike manner: "What a heaven she lived in!" (58). In her relationship with the Red Girl, Annie does not, as with Gwen, seek a lost ideal. Rather, she repeats a relationship that is—ironically, since the Red Girl is prized for being everything the mother would hate—similar to the relationship between Annie and her mother. Like the mother, the Red Girl is sure of her own power in her relationship with Annie; hence, she is the one to be courted. She accepts Annie's gifts carelessly, and sometimes, like the mother, seems to love and hate Annie at the same time, first pinching her until she cries and then kissing the painful places. And Annie has developed a taste for this kind of treatment: "Oh, the sensation was delicious—the combination of pinches and kisses. . . . I stopped wondering why all the girls whom I had mistreated and abandoned followed me around with looks of love and adoration on their faces" (63). No longer a little girl living in love's paradise, Annie must now learn about love's cruelty as well.

The Red Girl also represents the possibility of courage and vision, qualities missing from the increasingly controlled sphere of Annie and her mother. With the fearless Red Girl in the lead, Annie climbs to the frightening heights of the forbidden lighthouse. The girls survey sea and land from its top in a scene reminiscent of a moment in Annie's favorite novel, *Jane Eyre*. Jane, like Annie, is struggling to find her own way in life, and climbs to the battlements of Thornfield Hall, looking out to the horizon, and "long[ing] for a power of vision . . . which might reach the busy world, towns, regions full of life I had heard of but never seen" (140).

The Red Girl further helps to broaden Annie's horizons by introducing the unladylike and forbidden game of marbles. Since her mother so explicitly disapproves of marbles, Annie plays secretly and obsessively, devoting all her free time to the game, playing in a way "that I had never done anything" (61). Through the Red Girl's agency, Annie, for the first time, discovers something in herself that has not been fostered by, and is not sanctioned by, her mother.

Ironically, it is Annie's mother who gives her her first marbles, which have come as the prize in a package of oats. But this is just another example of the mother opening up a world only to try to take it away. Indeed, the marbles the mother gives Annie resemble the world, "the

white representing the seas, the colors representing the land masses"
(55). When Annie's mother accuses Annie of playing marbles and crawls
under the house to search furiously for them, she is seeking out the new
world Annie is building for herself.

Significantly, the mother cannot find the marbles, though they are
right under her hand. Blinded by her fury at being defied, she has lost
her ability to see the child at all. Annie's mother then shifts strategies,
seeking to cajole an admission from Annie by telling a story of her own
girlhood, about a trip down a mountain with a basket of figs on her
head. By the time she reached the bottom, the load, which had grown
heavier and heavier, was revealed to contain a very long black snake, and
the girl collapsed in horror. As the mother hopes, Annie is very much
moved by this story, feeling as though her "heart would break" (69).
Surely she identifies with the young girl and her horror at discovering a
hidden enemy. But of course Annie's hidden enemy is her mother, and
just as Annie is about to give up her marble collection, the mother figuratively becomes the snake in the garden, saying in a voice that is "warm
and soft and treacherous . . . 'Well, Little Miss, where are your marbles?'" Quickly Annie remembers herself and, demonstrating that she
continues to learn the lessons her mother teaches, replies in her "own
warm, soft, and newly acquired treacherous voice . . . 'I don't have any
marbles. I have never played marbles you know'" (70).

Now the Red Girl, having served her purpose of helping to push
Annie's relationship with her mother to its inevitable breaking point,
disappears from Annie's world; so does Annie's interest in marbles.
Childish rebellion is not the answer; it is only a step along the way to
finding a new world. Still, Annie allows herself one last Red Girl fantasy,
for we see that the Red Girl, in being paradoxically different from yet
similar to the mother, represents Annie's continued yearning for her
mother's love. In Annie's fantasy—echoing the one at the end of
Kincaid's story "In the Night"—she saves the Red Girl from a shipwreck
and "[takes] her to an island, where [they live] together forever" (71).
The two send "confusing signals," causing the destruction of cruise ships
that pass. European conquest and colonial empire, represented by the
ships, have confused the signals between Annie and her mother, causing
their love to founder, and their "cries of joy" turn to "cries of sorrow"
(71), like those of the people aboard the ships.

In the preceding chapter, the Red Girl and her marbles had helped to
precipitate a crisis between Annie and her mother. Now mother and
daughter are acknowledged enemies in a power struggle over Annie's

future and even her soul. For the moment, however, Kincaid turns from the mother-daughter relationship to focus on Annie and her studies, particularly the study of history, again suggesting the connection between European dominance and mother-daughter disharmony, for Annie's relationship with her mother mirrors the relationship between colonized and colonizer. Both at home and at school, particularly in history class, Annie is expected to empathize with a power that is determined to quash her individuality and make her into a flattering mirror of itself. So confident is this expectation on the part of the colonial school system that the children, including Annie, are confused about where they stand. The children know they are descendants of those enslaved by the British, but they have been so thoroughly taught to celebrate the British Empire that they cannot help feeling themselves to be on the side of empire: "Sometimes, what with our teachers and our books, it was hard for us to tell on which side we really now belonged—with the masters or the slaves—for it was all history, it was all in the past, and everybody behaved differently now" (76).

As Annie's conflict with her mother intensifies, however, she gains an insight into the workings of manipulative power in other spheres. She begins to see how a ᵘⁿ can manipulate the way in which things are perceived. She not ᵉ ample, how something degrading can be made to look like a prize, observing that the dunce cap, a badge of shame worn by girls who have not learned their lessons, is really quite beautiful, shaped like a coronet, covered with shiny gold paper and shiny red lettering. "When the sun shone on it the dunce cap was all aglitter, almost as if you were being tricked into thinking it was a desirable thing to wear" (75).

She sees, too, that one may be called upon to revere certain figures not because they deserve it or are truly superhuman, but because they want one's unquestioning support of their often questionable actions. Thus, Annie is able to see through the adoration the children are taught to feel for Columbus, portrayed in her history books as a sort of god who created the West Indies with his discovery. Her new insight into the workings of manipulative power allows Annie to see Columbus quite differently—as a grandiose tyrant. The full-color picture meant to inspire pity—Columbus being sent back to Spain in chains—strikes Annie as "just deserts" (77). She takes pleasure in seeing him "brought so low" (78). Connecting him with a tyrannical parent, she writes under the picture of Columbus words she has recently heard her mother use about her own overbearing but now incapacitated father: "The Great Man Can No

Longer Get Up And Go" (78). Showing a growing understanding of the methods of power, Annie writes the words in Old English script, thus clothing her "blasphemy" (82), as a teacher calls it, in the semblance of time-honored and even religious truth.

Her punishment is fitting and represents a warning of what will happen to Annie if she continues with her blasphemies. For defaming one of the empire's great men, she is required to pay homage to another great man, John Milton, by copying out the first two books of *Paradise Lost*. Further, Milton's work tells the story of Lucifer, who dares to challenge unchallengeable authority and who is, in punishment, cast out of paradise, plunged into a blackness of despair and eternal exile. Returning home after receiving this punishment, Annie hopes for some solace, but instead is met with yet another manipulative ploy as her mother presents her with a new dish, "a new kind of rice imported from Belgium" (83). The food smells exactly like the common breadfruit, which Annie hates, and she is never in any doubt that it is the despised breadfruit, as the mother later admits it to be. Clearly, Annie is losing the capacity to be duped, to accept a thing as something it is not. A hateful thing is still hateful, even when adorned with the European glitter by which colonial peoples have been methodically bedazzled.

In the previous chapters Annie has struggled to deny, and then rebel against, the change she has perceived in her world, the loss of childhood paradise, of which she seemed to be the beloved center. Finally, however, Annie's denials and rebellions can no longer hold up against the tide of grief that has been building as she comes to see that the world around her has grown murderous, intent on killing all that is authentic within her. As Annie slides into the collapse of "The Long Rain" chapter, grief begins to collect like a "mist," blotting out the world.

The horror of the change that has come over the world can no longer be avoided. While Annie and her mother both arrange a "face" for her father and the rest of the world to see, showing themselves to be as loving to one another as ever, they no longer pretend when they are alone. Then "everything darken[s]" and Annie feels "something I could not name just [came] over us" (88). In recurring dreams Annie hears herself chant, "My mother would kill me if she got the chance. I would kill my mother if I had the courage" (89).

The world of school and friends no longer provides a hopeful alternative to the mother's world, since the older girls with whom Annie now associates do not dread "the future full of ridiculous demands" (53) as her younger schoolmates did; no longer do they cavort sacrilegiously on the tombstones of their former masters. Rather, they primp and pose, insult and compete, appearing to have sold themselves entirely to win scraps of official favor. Even Gwen, once so belovedly herself, has become "a bundle of who said what and who did what" (92). The girls have lost themselves without even noticing, and to Annie, they are hopelessly dull: "They had no different ideas of how to be in the world; they certainly didn't think that the world was a strange place to be caught living in" (90).

Annie has been spiritually deserted by both her mother and her young friends, and the world seems to reflect back to her only the image of her own oddness. Thus, when she sees her reflection in a store window, she does not at first recognize herself; she does not see herself as a real person, taking herself to be one of the things "just hanging there" among the bolts of cloth and household items. If the world seems to see her as an oddity, it also sees her, as does her mother, as a kind of criminal, and now the reflection in the window reminds Annie of a painting entitled *The Young Lucifer*, which shows Satan pretending bravado but really "lonely and miserable at the way things had turned out" (95).

The reflection in the window is also seen by some older boys standing across the street, who, recognizing and mocking the lonely "oddness" that is now Annie's face to the world, maliciously address her with exaggerated courtesy. As the boys mock her, Annie recognizes one of them, a former playmate, who always assigned himself all the roles in plays they would make up, leaving Annie to play "a person who fetched things" (96); he had once induced her to take off her clothes and sit on a nest of ants. Clearly, Annie is not to be saved from the betrayal of women by the chivalry of men.

On her way home, Annie experiences a sense of physical disorientation that heralds the breakdown to come. In a scene reminiscent of Lewis Carroll's *Alice's Adventures in Wonderland*, Annie feels herself grow "alternately too big and too small" (101). Alice grows too small to reach the key that could provide for her escape and then too large to fit through the unlocked door; Annie, alternating between childhood and womanhood, is both too large and too small to get through any of the available doors.[8]

She finds out when she gets home that someone else has observed her gazing into the store window, her mother, who was inside shopping. But her mother has not actually seen the girl; rather, the mother has projected upon the girl the vision of criminal puberty that seems to obsess her. She has thus not seen a sad young girl being cruelly mocked by malicious boys. Rather, she sees a "slut" who is "making a spectacle of [herself]" (102). Annie, "drowning" in this repeated, ridiculous accusation, hurls her own ridiculous accusation, "Well . . . like mother like daughter" (102). And the earth suddenly seems to "[fall] silent. The two black things joined together in the middle of the room [separate], hers going to her, mine coming to me. I looked at my mother. She seemed tired and old and broken" (102). For the first time, Annie has struck a telling blow against her mother as, heartbreakingly, she discovers the secret at the heart of her mother's betrayal. The mother not only betrays the girl but betrays herself in seeing maturity as a crime. The daughter's accusation, absurd though it seems, has such impact because, on some level, the mother understands it as the truth, for it is not really the girl whom the mother sees through the window but herself, her own reflection, as cast back to her by a society that sees black people, if not as children, then as devils.

With this seemingly accidental stroke, Annie has pierced the pretense of maternal moral nurture and the myth of her own culpability. And, as if partially freed by this revelation, she makes the first sad step toward departure. She requests that her father build her a new trunk to replace the mother's trunk, the one that now holds all of Annie's things. She is not sure but that, for the rest of her life, her mother's shadow will stand "between [her] and the rest of the world" (107), but knows finally that her life cannot be contained within her mother's.

In a chapter that seems to correspond roughly to the "Blackness" chapter in *At the Bottom of the River*, Annie suffers a mental and physical collapse, feels blotted out by "blackness." A "black thing" is inside her head, shutting out her "memory of the things that happened to me," and she dreams that she is walking "through warm air filled with soot" (112). Her collapse is accompanied by a three-month rain, during which the seas rise and "dry land is covered with water." After the rain, "in spite of what everyone said, the sea never did go back to the way it had been" (109). Attributed to overwork at school or an obeah spell, the collapse is certainly the result of Annie's sense of grievous loss and a step in her mourning process. Her illness echoes the biblical flood sent to punish the wicked—accompanied as it is by the long rain and the rising seas—washing away all but the just. The deluge figuratively washes away a life that has become too painful, clearing the way for a rebirth. When the rain ends, some things, "in spite of what everyone said," are changed forever, and one of them is Annie, who assumes her own name. No longer is she Little Miss, as her parents and everyone else call her.

In this flood many things once taken for granted are uprooted. Language, for instance, shows itself to be without inherent meaning but dependent on a cooperative listener. Words leave Annie's parents' mouths, "[travel] through the air toward me, but just as they reached my ears they would fall to the floor, suddenly dead" (109). Childhood activities and efforts, too, as symbolized by Annie's eager participation in the Brownie Scouts, with all their emblems, badges, and rituals, break away from any order or meaning. Now, in a fever dream, Annie sees her Brownie self reduced to a tiny toy, utterly trivialized.

That the illness is like the biblical flood, in which all that was false or wicked was washed away, is borne out by Annie's treatment of the photographs that sit on her bedside table. They also seem to be suffering a breakdown, as they, too, Alice-like, "began to blow themselves up until they touched the ceiling and then shrink back down, but to a size that I could not easily see" (119). They do this until they are so limp with exhaustion and reeking with perspiration that Annie decides they need washing. What Annie claims to be doing is setting the photographs to rights, straightening her aunt's wedding veil, getting the dirt off her father's trousers. But, in fact, she is trying to wash away the falseness and vileness of the world. She obliterates all the faces but her own in the wedding party photograph, for everyone she knows seems guilty of falseness, betraying their own and Annie's true selves. As they seem to have erased her, she now erases them. In another photograph, she erases her mother and father "from the waist down" (120), for maturity and its accompanying sexuality appear to have caused most of the trouble in Annie's world. In the picture of herself in her confirmation dress, she has erased everything but the shoes with "decorative cutouts on the side" (118), which represent an "enormous fight" with her mother over appropriate wear for a "young lady" (119). Now Annie and her white confirmation dress have all been washed away; nothing is left but her feet in the defiant shoes. Annie's participation in the rituals of her childhood life has come to be seen as a kind of self-betrayal; all that she really has of herself now is her refusal to be made over in someone else's image, even if this refusal can as yet take no more significant form than fancy shoes.

Finally, as the rains fall and the sea rises, as the old ways, even the old loves, are washed away, Annie is being prepared for rebirth, which is assisted by her magical maternal grandmother, Ma Chess, an obeah woman who knows "at least ten times more" than the local obeah practitioner, Ma Jolie (123). It is appropriate that Ma Chess arrive on this flood (she does not come, in the ordinary way, on the steamer), for she is a woman who is intimately familiar with the regenerative powers of water, who bathes in a special bath "in which things animal and vegetable had been boiled for a long time" and who prepares for this bath by first swimming in the sea (124).

Ma Chess knows what it is to lose a child to a mysterious illness; her son Johnny, Annie's uncle, died in his youth, apparently the result of an obeah curse. Following his death, Ma Chess kept all of his things in a large trunk, sometimes showing "all of it as if it were part of a great exhibition" (124). But Ma Chess immediately pronounces that Annie is "not like Johnnie. Not like Johnnie at all" (124). She is not doomed by some mysterious curse; she has not died, physically or spiritually; she will be more than the contents of a mother's trunk.

Ma Chess was apparently not able to save her own child's life, only his death, as witnessed by his containment in the trunk. Perhaps Kincaid is saying that at some point, mothers cannot save their children, cannot even see them, and this task must fall to another, for Ma Chess sees immediately the cause of the child's illness, that she needs to be remothered until she finds a sense of self again: "Sometimes at night, when I would feel that I was all locked up in the warm falling soot and could not find my way out, Ma Chess would come into my bed with me and stay until I was myself—whatever that had come to be by then—again" (125–26). Indeed, with Ma Chess, Annie seems to be taken back into the womb, as she lies beside her grandmother, "curled up like a little comma" (126).

The rain ends, the illness subsides, Ma Chess departs as magically as she has come. Some things, washed away in the long rain—such as Annie's mother's garden and the foundation of a house her father was building—can be restored; others cannot, at least not in Annie's present life. Any simple attachment to her mother and her home has gone, as has any sense of being part of the world in which she was born. Annie is not happy, but she is stable. No longer does she expand and shrink; rather, she has grown "to a considerable height," now "towering" over her mother. She has thoroughly accepted her sense of being "odd," different from everyone, and she does everything she can to enhance it, dressing, walking, and talking oddly, purposely creating "such a picture that apparently everyone talked about me" (128). Everything has washed away, except that part of her that is defiantly at odds with everything around her. Everything she does and says grates against the sensibilities of those around her, and for the present, this is her only happiness.

"My name is Annie John" are the opening words of her book's final chapter. Annie's name, painted in large letters on her new trunk, is the last thing she sees before falling asleep and the first thing she thinks of when she wakes on the morning of her departure from Antigua. She is leaving, not because she wants to go to England or to study to be a nurse, as is planned; she is leaving because departure is the only way to preserve a precarious, newborn sense of identity. So thoroughly has her world betrayed her—refusing to see her except as a reflection of itself—that even the once-beloved objects of her room seem to be part of the betrayal and she feels that her heart could "burst open with joy" (132) at never having to see any of the familiar things or people of her life again.

Even on the morning of her departure the world around her continues to assert itself, to reach out to control her future, still certain that she is its reflection, entirely responsive to its sense of life's forces. An obeah woman has done "whatever she had done" to Annie's jewelry and underclothes to protect her from "evil spirits and every kind of misfortune" (134). Her mother knowingly suggests that Annie will soon marry. Friends who come by mention both her glorious future achievements that will credit them all and the sorrow that her departure will cause those left behind.

But, as the moment of departure draws near, she is torn again between the love she has had for these people and this place and the sense of betrayal she feels. As she walks with her parents to the jetty, she remembers without irony her life before the fall from grace. Now making what she believes will be her last walk along the road, she remembers her first, when, as a five-year-old, she was allowed to go to the store unaccompanied with three pennies in her market basket. When she returned with her packages, her mother's eyes filled with tears as she pronounced the girl "wonderful and good and that there would never by anybody better. If I had just conquered Persia, she couldn't have been more proud of me" (140). This is a memory of a lost past, but it is also a vision of an undiscovered future, for Annie is determined to find a way to see herself as "wonderful and good" again, to become again the conqueror of new worlds.

At the moment of departure, the pain of loss and the triumph of renewal momentarily coexist; she is both dying and coming alive: "Suddenly a wave of strong feeling came over me, and my heart swelled with a great gladness as the words 'I shall never see this again' spilled out inside me. But then, just as quickly, my heart shriveled up and the words 'I shall never see this again' stabbed at me" (145). Moved, Annie and her mother cry, and her mother holds her so tightly that she cannot breathe. Annie is suddenly "on [her] guard," remembering that the price of this love is death by suffocation (147).

In the book's last image, Annie goes to her cabin and lies down in her berth, and then hears a sound "as if a vessel filled with liquid had been placed on its side and now was slowly emptying out" (148). There is a desolation in the image of the vessel left on its own, its contents dribbling out to no particular purpose. It can be read as an image of death, as the blood flows from the body. But it is also an image of impending renewal, for if the vessel is not too fragile to sustain its own emptiness, the old makes way for the new.

Chapter Eight
Lucy: In the New World

Jamaica Kincaid's second novel, *Lucy*, is a continuation of the bil-dungsroman begun with *Annie John*, although the name of the protago-nist has been changed. *Annie John* closes with the young Annie leaving Antigua for England and a nursing career. The second book opens with a teenager named Lucy arriving in an unnamed American city that resem-bles New York, where she will work as a nanny for a well-to-do family. In both books, then, Kincaid sends her young heroines on the first of the journeys usually made by the protagonists in West Indian novels, according to Daryl Cumber Dance, into the "white Western world."[1]

The West Indian author's dramatis personae often make three jour-neys, Dance writes, "starting with the journey to England (or more recently the United States or Canada) [which generally] reinforces the fact that the cold and alien land is not home and that the traveller must divest himself of his Europeanization or his Westernization" (18). The second journey, Dance says, is to Africa (or India); the third is a return to the West Indian home. This last journey often reveals that the author and his protagonist have become, through education and contact with the metropolis, too different from the person they once were to fit in at home; they have been taken too far from "their people, their roots and thus themselves" (19).

On arriving in the wintry American city, Lucy does indeed feel herself to be in a "cold and alien land," in a place that decidedly is not home. In the frigid North American January, where it is freezing even when the sun is shining, she feels, for the first time in her life, cold both "inside and out" (6). So bleak does the future look—"a gray blank, an overcast seascape on which rain was falling and no boats were in sight" (6)—that the unhappiness of her island girlhood makes her "happy now just to think of it," for it is so "familiar and predictable" (5–6).

Lucy initially finds the new land "cold and alien," but she does not, I believe, come to any realizations about "divesting" herself of "Europeanization" or "Westernization." Rather, it is possible to see in Kincaid's work a philosophy similar to that expounded by Françoise Lionnet, herself a native of the long-colonized island country of Mauritius.

Lionnet suggests that the very idea of essential racial, sexual, geographic, or cultural oppositions is the product of a European worldview predicated on the existence and manipulation of hierarchical relationships (9). By this reasoning, to attempt to divest oneself of Europeanization would be to accept a philosophical system of hierarchical division. To do so would be, as Lionnet puts it, to engage hegemonic power "on its own terms" and then to become "a term within that system of power" (6).

Lionnet's thinking helps us read Kincaid, for in *Lucy* she does not show her protagonist attempting to choose between two identities. This does not indicate that Lucy is unaware of the dichotomy. She is quite aware of the two options most readily available to her: to remain in a place where she cannot really be at home or to journey to a place where she will be a vulnerable outsider. These options are clarified by a letter from her mother that details the "horrible and vicious" things that happened to "an immigrant girl" of Lucy's exact age who had had her throat cut in a North American underground train (21). While Lucy does not discount this and is actually made "afraid to even put my face outside the door," she also understands that "real fear" can exist at home too and tells the story of a girl of Lucy's age who was beaten by her father, who "had dealings with the Devil" (21). The only way the girl could escape was to cross the sea, since "the Devil cannot walk over water." Presumably though, once the girl had crossed the sea, she would be subject to having her throat cut by criminals. While Lucy sees the invitation to choose between self-torment at home and the violence of an alien metropolis, she refuses to accept that these are the only two choices: "I thought, On the one hand there was a girl being beaten by a man she could not see; on the other there was a girl getting her throat cut by a man she could see. In this great big world, why should my life be reduced to these two possibilities?" (21).

Lucy thus rejects the available identities offered by her mother and Antiguan society, the British Empire, her well-meaning employer Mariah, the American man who finds her exotic, and her employers' African-American maid, who thinks her manner of speaking and acting is disgustingly prim and proper. What all of these seem to offer Lucy is a role, based on their perception of her place in a framework of "essential oppositions," whether "racial, cultural, sexual or geographical." Since Lucy's first task of self-definition is to reject proffered roles, the sense of self is first formed in the negative. The self is, first, that which resists easily accessible identity, that which can separate itself from the narcissistic pull of powerful forces. Thus, Lucy's clearest statement of her new iden-

tity, formed during her first year in America, is in the negative: "I had
been a girl of whom certain things were expected, none of them too bad:
a career as a nurse, for example; a sense of duty to my parents; obedience
to the law and worship of convention. But in one year of being away
from home, that girl had gone out of existence" (133). Lucy cannot say
what exactly will come to replace that girl. She only knows that she is
following a powerful instinct to find a self that feels authentic: "I understood that I was inventing myself more in the way of a painter than in
the way of a scientist. I could not count on precision or calculation; I
could only count on intuition. I did not have anything exactly in mind,
but when the picture was complete I would know. I did not have position, I did not have money at my disposal. I had memory, I had anger, I
had despair" (134). Like Lucifer, for whom she is named, she has lost
much, if not all, she has ever loved. Rather than finding herself trapped
between worlds, she finds herself with no world at all. All she has left,
like Lucifer, is an "unconquerable will" and "courage never to submit or
yield" (Milton, 1.106, 108).

Much of what she must never "submit or yield" to still emanates from
her home, where her mother remains dominant. Although Lucy has
escaped her mother's literal reach, she has not escaped the magnetic field
of her mother's power. If anything, the mother's power grows even larger when viewed from a distance; she seems to be "a god," not a human.
So intense is the mother's pull on the lonely, still unformed girl that Lucy
does not dare to open her mother's letters, knowing that "if I read only
one, I would die from longing for her" (91).

Set apart from her old world as Lucy now is, and not yet a part of the
new, she can see the manipulative power of both empire and the "white
West" quite clearly. At home she two-facedly memorized an ode to the
daffodil, a flower beloved by the British but never seen by West Indian
children. On being shown her first daffodil, Lucy reacts with single-
minded fury, understanding it to be a brilliantly disguised weapon of
imperial domination, subtly and disarmingly advancing the notion that
everything European is better than anything found in the West Indies.

While Annie John only slowly comes to understand the hypocrisy
that is the underpinning of her world—benevolence based on the
assumption of, and desire for, power rather than on true love and gen-
erosity—Lucy has a newcomer's quick eye for contradictions. She studies her happy, affectionate employer, Mariah, for example, always aware
of the gap that exists between Mariah's desire to be loving and sympathetic and her understanding of what life is for people less privileged

than herself. The people Lucy encounters in America are usually white and friendly. But despite their friendliness, they, like the mother and colonial culture, can be dangerous to the girl's search for identity, for they, too, often see her as someone to use narcissistically, to reflect their own preferred image back to them, rather than as someone who exists exclusively as and for herself. Thus, Mariah seeks to help Lucy over her sadness and loss by offering books on feminism, books that may be significant to Mariah but have very little relevance to Lucy's own situation. Lucy's lover, Paul, likewise sees in her the embodiment of romantic and tragic mystery. Whether he understands it or not, she knows that to him she is a kind of artifact, mirroring his taste back to him. For Lucy's friend and roommate, the Irish-American Peggy, she is valuable insofar as she reflects and supports Peggy's own rebellion against family and propriety. Lucy risks Peggy's disapproval, however, if she ever steps out of this role.

While most people Lucy encounters are white, Kincaid has drawn at the beginning of the book one of its few apparently black American characters, Mariah's maid, who does not like the newcomer because she "spoke like a nun" and because "everything about [Lucy] was so pious it made her feel at once sick to her stomach and sick with pity" (11). The woman is sure that Lucy cannot dance but still shares the latest hit record—sung by a girl group resembling the Supremes—which Lucy finds to have a "shallow" melody and "meaningless" words. Indeed, Lucy "can't join" the woman as she magnificently dances, and Lucy's rendition of a calypso number does not seem to change the fact that she makes the other woman "sick to her stomach" (12). If the old world sought to define Kincaid's protagonist in terms of an internalized cultural, racial, and sexual hierarchy, the new world seeks to appropriate her as a reflection of, or trophy to, its own values. This seems to hold for white and black alike.

In the end, Lucy wins no ringing victory in her attempt to "invent" herself. The "shadow" of the mother, which Annie feared might always stand "between [her] and the rest of the world" (*AJ*, 107), still looms, though it no longer blots out the world. Like Annie John, Lucy has tried to draw a picture of herself by inspecting herself in a variety of relationships. Relationships with Gwen, the Red Girl, and school friends allowed Annie to act out aspects of her relationship with her mother, her desire for perfect union, and her desire to rebel. In *Lucy* something similar happens, as relationships with Mariah and Peggy allow Lucy to act out parts of herself, the part that still wants a loving mother figure and the part that wants to rebel against every propriety. But here, as in *Annie John*,

Kincaid's protagonist learns that she will ultimately have to go on alone if she is to form an authentic picture of herself. Lucy cannot trust even Hugh, the one character who seems to see her as something other than a reflection of himself, not to interfere.

The first chapter of *Lucy* presents a young West Indian girl entering into what she believes will be a permanent exile. Though she has been unhappy at home—readers of *Annie John* are acquainted with this unhappiness—that sorrow is now a cherished memory when compared with the cold, gray emptiness of the world now facing her.

Lucy is given a small, high-ceilinged room that reminds her of "a box in which cargo traveling a long way should be shipped." She is struck by this image even though she is, as she says, not cargo, "only an unhappy young woman" (7). The danger that confronts Lucy, set out at the book's very beginning, is that she will become cargo, that she will be valued in this new world as a kind of exotic possession, if not as a slave, then as a kind of curio, an object in either case.

Lucy is treated kindly by her well-to-do employers and their four children, a laughing and beautiful family. Their six yellow-haired heads remind her of a "bouquet of flowers" (12), and at the same time that Lucy appreciates their apparently innocent beauty, she also sees that they, like the daffodils in the poem she was forced to memorize at home, embody the "white Western world" that the West Indian child has been taught to value at the expense of her love for her own world. Instinctively, Lucy sees the friendly family as a threat, fearing that whoever her emerging self turns out to be, it may not hold up under the friendly onslaught of this confident and energetic family. A dream reflects this fear as bunches of daffodils chase Lucy until she is exhausted, and then pile on top of her, burying her so that she is "never seen again" (18).

Sensing, perhaps, Lucy's need to hold herself a little apart, her employers, in their friendly fashion, soon begin to joke about her reserve, to call her "Visitor," for they say that she "seemed not to be a part of things, as if [she] didn't live in their house with them, as if they weren't like a family to [her]" (13). Lewis, the father of the family, tells a story about an uncle who went away to raise monkeys and finally got so used to them that he preferred them to people. The moral seems to be that Lucy will grow so used to this charming family, however strange it may initially seem, that she will come to prefer them to the sort of people she used to know.

Lucy replies with a story of her own, a dream in which she runs naked as Lewis chases her and Mariah, his wife, calls, "Catch her." Finally, Lucy falls down a hole "at the bottom of which were some silver and blue snakes" (14). The story temporarily silences the talkative family, until Lewis and Mariah find a sexual interpretation. "Dr. Freud for Visitor," Mariah says, and they laugh in a "soft, kind way" (15). Kincaid's narrator says that the dream shows only that she has "taken them in, because only people who were very important to me had ever shown up in my dreams" (15).

But while the dream may hint of sexual desire and certainly shows that the family has entered Lucy's subconscious, another explanation seems unavoidable. The family's teasing and Lewis's story both suggest that Lucy should be subsumed into the family, that she should drop her sense of difference or separateness, that she should become like them, that she should *be* them as nearly as possible. Some part of Lucy recognizes this invitation to imitate her employers as something very familiar, for, particularly if we read *Lucy* in light of *Annie John*, we know that a similar invitation—no regrets allowed—was a central feature of the previous world. Both Annie's mother and the colonial authorities taught that she should first adore them and then, in the sincerest form of flattery, strive to become them or as nearly like them as possible. If Lewis's story speaks finally of narcissistic domination, Lucy's dream is about evasion. Lewis chases her around the house; Mariah urges him on. They are determined to possess her. Lucy runs, vulnerable and naked, having shed her old identity but not yet having found anything with which to replace it. Though she runs, there is really no escape, as she is trapped in Lewis and Mariah's world. The only escape is for the earth to open up and swallow her, and that is what it does as Lucy falls down a hole.

At least subconsciously, Lucy refuses to exchange one form of domination for another, and so she dreams herself into another, magical dimension, one in which old power equations are broken. If her fall down a hole is an echo of Alice's fall in *Alice's Adventures in Wonderland*, then we may see that the new dimension, though disorienting, also holds out promise. In it, as Alice says, "so many out-of-the-way things" happen that one may begin to think that "very few things indeed were really impossible."[2]

In the book's first chapter, Lucy not only feels herself to be lost and naked in a cold dark world but also sees in the new landscape a threatening hint that the attempt to define herself will be overwhelmed by the assumption of her employers that she will, more or less, become one of them. In the second chapter, this theme is broadened as Lucy studies her employer, Mariah. If the family seems to embody the supposedly perfect white world that West Indian children have been taught to admire from a distance, Mariah seems to represent the best possible individual example of that world. She is kind and loving toward Lucy, wanting to include her in everything and to introduce her to new pleasures, whether they be the first daffodils of spring or a first overnight train ride. No soulless, urban materialist, Mariah glories in her children, in the beauty and rhythm of nature, and in the simple pleasures of her childhood home on the Great Lakes. She seems happiest when she is in her kitchen, arranging plants with her large capable hands and, in this, resembles Lucy's mother at her best.

Kincaid's creation of this character tells us something important about her investigation of the white Western world. The threat to Lucy does not come in the form of racists, either crude or subtle, for these do not appear in her work. Even class discrimination, practiced by those friends of Mariah who see Lucy as merely "the girl who takes care of the children" (58), is placed in the background as a kind of minor irritation. As noted earlier, Lucy refuses to see the "great big world" as defined in two simple terms: self-hatred at home and hatred abroad. Rather, the threat to Lucy and to the self she is trying to create will not arise out of violence or hatred but from those who possess many admirable and even lovable qualities and who reach out in friendship. In the world of Kincaid's protagonists, the great danger is not in overt hostility and brutality but in being presented with something that you will love too much and, through that love, be lost to yourself.

To confront this greatest danger, Kincaid creates the kind and loving Mariah, a woman who seems to have every good quality, against whom Lucy must define herself. To study what Mariah is, and what she is not, Lucy summons up a memory of her mother's friend Sylvie, who had a rose-shaped scar on her cheek where she had been bitten by another woman in a quarrel over a man. As a child, Lucy understood the mark as symbolizing the "heavy and hard" beginning of "living, really living," and the girl is sure she will "end up with a mark somewhere" (25). This, Lucy concludes, is what separates her from Mariah. Mariah is unmarked by life, by the ferocious struggle of love and loss. It as if she has remained in the blissful childhood from which Lucy's predecessor, Annie John, was so painfully wrenched. For Mariah's life to be so clear and simple, free of doubt or even of "confidence," Lucy believes, "things must have always gone her way, and not just for her but for everybody she has ever known from eternity; she has never had to doubt, and so she has never had to grow confident; the right thing always happens to her; the thing she wants to happen happens" (26).

Like the beautiful daffodils, which "looked simple, as if made to erase a complicated and unnecessary idea" (29), Mariah's existence seems to invalidate the complication and difficulty of Lucy's life. Conversely, if Lucy's experience is to be valid, then Mariah's simple assumptions must be invalidated. And so, as Lucy is overcome with the "mysterious" desire to kill the daffodils, she also demonstrates a determination to demolish Mariah's innocence, to insist that life is in fact complicated, much more so than Mariah has yet grasped. Thus, she complicates Mariah's appreciation of the daffodils by showing how they were used to make West Indian children love a world in which they could never belong. And Lucy deflates Mariah's simple joy in the sight of freshly plowed fields out the train window as they travel toward Mariah's childhood home on one of the Great Lakes. She reminds Mariah of the historical link between physical labor and domination based on race, remarking with "a cruel tone" in her voice, "Well, thank God I didn't have to do that" (33)—this after Mariah has failed to notice that the railway dining car is filled with diners who look like her and who are being served by waiters who look like Lucy.

Mariah's sense of her own entitlement grows as she, the children, and Lucy draw nearer to their summer home. Growing along with it is her desire that others, particularly Lucy and the children, see and love things in just the way that she does. Mariah unites within herself the sense of ownership that comes of privilege and a maternal attitude that reminds Lucy of her own mother. As in *Annie John*, Kincaid makes a connection between the dominant cultural group and her mother; both narcissistically insist on being favorably reflected by those in their power. And so, while Mariah's own children are willing to see things their mother's way, Lucy, struggling with Mariah's combination of cultural and maternal power, is not. Mariah's wish reminds her of her feeling "that my mother's love for me was designed solely to make me into an echo of her; and I didn't know why, but I felt that I would rather be dead than become just an echo of someone" (36).

Lucy continues to insist on seeing Mariah in a light other than Mariah's own. When Mariah is applauding herself for catching some fish, dancing, and singing, "I will make you fishers of men," Lucy deflates both Mariah and Jesus by telling a story of her own childhood wherein she responded to the story of Jesus and the loaves by asking, "But how did Jesus serve the fish? Boiled or fried?" (38). Neither Mariah nor Jesus, the story implies, is so miraculous as to escape life's tiresome little details.

Lucy manages to shake Mariah's innocent view of the world and to undermine her ability to separate herself from the reality of other peoples' experience. Mariah still confides to Lucy that she has a little "Indian blood," something Mariah has been "looking forward" to doing, but now she is unsure, fearing that Lucy will "take it the wrong way." When Lucy responds coldly, Mariah's expression is one of anguish. Yet Lucy's "triumph" is hollow. Mariah's simplicity must be shaken so that it cannot threaten the validity of Lucy's complex experience. Still, there is a sadness, as Kincaid's protagonists know only too well, in any loss of innocence.

If the first two chapters of *Lucy* revolve around Lucy's fear of once more being robbed of herself as a result of pressure to emulate and reflect others, in the book's third chapter Lucy begins to find her balance, strengthened in part by the simple fact of having survived on her own for six months. Still, she views the new world largely in terms of life at home. She is frightened, for example, of the wooded area separating the family's summer home from the lake, since she imagines unknown beings lurking there. She is still very much of a place where people believe in obeah, where "there was no such thing as a 'real' thing, because often what seemed to be one thing turned out to be altogether different" (54). But though she is frightened, Lucy continues to walk through the woods, and eventually grows less fearful, beginning to see "something beautiful about it" (55). Although fear is still there, Lucy is discovering that it need not be crippling.

And while, in the previous chapter, Lucy was determined to shake her employer's simple, sunny view of the world, now she has less need to force uncomfortable connections on Mariah. Lucy refrains, for example, from pointing out that the environmental destruction Mariah decries may be related to the comforts she enjoys. The earlier need to deflate Mariah is, at least in part, an aspect of Lucy's continuing examination of her conflict with her mother and a reenactment of that conflict. That Lucy is able to succeed in shaking Mariah reveals that she is not, like Lucy's own mother, "large, like a god" (150); she is only human. As Lucy is able to hold her own, she gains a sense of her own power. Then, less threatened, she is able to view Mariah in a more rational light, discovering that while Mariah is sometimes guilty of a narcissistic inability to see the reality of others and of a desire that others see what she sees, she is also able at times to understand the separate needs of others. She despises Lucy's cynical friend Peggy, for example; nevertheless, she accepts Lucy's need for the friendship. In this way, Lucy says, "Mariah was superior to my mother, for my mother would never come to see that perhaps my needs were more important than her wishes" (63–64).

Thus, in casting Mariah as her mother, Lucy uses Mariah as a way of redefining herself against what has seemed a magical, omnipotent maternal power. Like the Michigan woods, Mariah at first seems to possess the sort of frightening magic Lucy knew at home. But, after a series of tests, Lucy finds that neither Mariah nor the forest has that sort of omnipotence; like the devil who cannot cross the sea, the fearsome magic of home has not accompanied her to the new environment. Lucy can remain intact in the face of her fears and, feeling her own new power, can even begin to see and enjoy the beauty in that which she had previously feared. Strangely, she is safer here than at home, where she was overwhelmed by magical and omnipotent forces.

There is another reason for Lucy's more protective attitude toward Mariah. Whereas at first Mariah's life appeared to be perfect, and Mariah a person who "had never had to doubt," since "the right thing always happens to her" (26), Lucy now sees that this is not really the case, for Lucy has become aware, though Mariah is still oblivious, that Mariah's husband is unfaithful to her and that Mariah's perfect life stands on a shaky foundation. Here Kincaid uses the character of Mariah in a different way. While she is cast, particularly in the previous chapter, as the representative of narcissistic power against whom Lucy must fight if she is to forge a separate identity, Mariah seems here to mirror Lucy herself, the child summarily expelled from a paradise of love. Further, while Lucy initially calls up the memory of Sylvie, a woman eternally scarred by the passions of love, as a counterpoint to the unblemished Mariah, we now see that Mariah and love-marked Sylvie have more in common than may have originally been thought. And so, while Lucy at first feels the need to ruffle the perfection of Mariah's life, she comes to see that this is not necessary, that even the "golden" and privileged Mariah cannot stay in paradise forever. Not only is she not magically powerful, but she is not magically spared life's difficulties.

As Lucy sees Mariah's life begin to unravel, she becomes less paralyzed by the grief over her own loss. Earlier, Lucy seemed crippled by the idea that there are two kinds of people, those marked for suffering and those who remain forever unblemished. Now, as even the most privi-

leged life is shaken, Lucy is able to see loss as part of the human condition, not as a special punishment reserved for those who somehow, like
Lucifer, have fallen. If Mariah and Lucy begin the book as gleaming God
and grieving Lucifer, they end it as a very different pair, a version of
Adam and Eve, both sadly making their way out of the garden of Eden.

In previous chapters, Lucy struggled to come to terms with the new
world and the new people she found in it. At first, she feared that she
would be somehow subsumed by these people who seemed so confident
in their own perfection. Or, if she could resist the pull to become them
or to be as like them as possible, she was threatened with the danger of
becoming an object, a piece of exotica, or a screen on which the people
she met could project their own emotions about racial and cultural difference.

But, as Lucy returns to the city after a summer in the country—a
summer during which she comes to understand that the perfect, "gold-
en" Mariah is not immune to life's grievous losses—she sees the new
world in a different light; she has "come to see the sameness in things
that appeared different" (91). Now that the shock of newness has worn
off and with it the fear that she will misplace her emerging self, she sees
that not only is the new world in some ways the same as the old, but she
herself is in many ways the same as she used to be: "As each day unfold-
ed before me, I could see the sameness in everything; I could see the present take a shape—the shape of my past" (90).

In "Cold Heart," then, the book takes a turn. Lucy is getting on her
feet in the new world. She is no longer awed and threatened by the
apparent perfection of lives in the white Western world. And the simple
fact of having survived for a time on her own, away from her mother, is
empowering. However, as Lucy's attention is no longer dominated by
her efforts to cope with the new world, it seems as if the force of her
mother, temporarily suppressed, now breaks through into Lucy's
American life. She has to suppress the mother's voice by saving, but not
reading, her letters, fearing that if she reads them she will "die from
longing for her" (91). Lucy begins to get violent headaches, just as her
mother used to do, especially when Lucy had done something to hurt
her. The headaches demonstrate Lucy's similarity to her mother—the
way in which she, as she says, *is* her mother—and may also be a sign of
Lucy's guilt for hurting her mother, this time for deserting her to go to
America. And a different type of recurrent dream begins. Whereas previously Lucy had repeatedly dreamed about the threatening nature of
her friendly American employers—of being buried by yellow-headed

daffodils, of being chased by Lewis as Mariah watched—she now dreams, over and over, of a wonderful gift wrapped in one of her mother's "beautiful madras head-kerchiefs" that lies at the bottom of a deep dark pool of water and that she can never reach before she awakens (87). Despite the distance she has traveled, Lucy is still the girl in *Annie John*, painfully separated from her beautiful, beloved mother by an insurmountable barrier.

As Annie John tries for a time to form a separate identity from her mother by befriending the Red Girl, Lucy, as she feels her mother's pull, repeats this strategy, taking up with Peggy, the Irish-American girl who, in her disdain for social propriety and good hygiene, would meet with the mother's thorough disapproval. Peggy is also attractive because her family has no "magical" hold over her; it merely irritates and bores her. Like the Red Girl, Peggy not only models defiant behavior but also helps broaden Lucy's horizons. The Red Girl introduces Annie to the forbidden but mesmerizing game of marbles; Peggy introduces Lucy to the pursuit most dreaded by Lucy's mother—sex for the fun of it, or, as the mother would put it, "sluttishness." Indeed, when Paul, the man to whom Peggy introduces Lucy, first looks at her across the room, his eyes remind her "of a marble I used to have, my lucky marble, the one that, when I played a game with it, always won" (99). Lucy knows that she is not in love, that she only wants to play, and her laugh is "shot full of pleasure and insincerity" (100). Finally, she has managed the greatest possible affront to her mother: she has delightedly become the "slut" her mother has always accused her of being.

There is another way in which sex with Paul is an attack on the mother's rule. When Lucy sees Paul's hands in a fish tank as he retrieves an earring, the flesh looks like bone, and she suddenly remembers a story from home: When a fisherman, Mr. Thomas, was drowned at sea, a girl named Myrna confessed to Annie that she often met Mr. Thomas in a dark alley, where "she would stand in the dark, fully clothed but without her panties, and he would put his middle finger up inside her" (104). Both the tough, cynical Myrna and the prim young Lucy see these encounters as immensely desirable; they make the otherwise downtrodden Myrna powerful and important. The meetings have a significance for the girls that goes far beyond the sixpences and shillings Mr. Thomas pays each time. In fact, Lucy is "overcome with jealousy" that "such an extraordinary thing" had not happened to her. With Lucy, of course, Mr. Thomas was the model of propriety, to the point of hiding his cigarette behind his back when she came to the door. He knows her to be "a teenage girl so beyond reproach in every way that if you asked her a question she would reply in her mother's forty-year-old voice—hardly a prospect for a secret rendezvous" (107). Now, with the help of Peggy, Lucy has found some of Myrna's rebellious toughness and her own Mr. Thomas. Sex with Paul is an assault on the mother's rule and also on the prim, mother-ridden girl Lucy has always been.

Lucy's magical mother, however, is not to be defeated so easily; her letters keep coming, including one marked "urgent." Lucy responds with defiance, not opening this letter but going out to buy a camera, thus seeking to shore up her own newfound method of fixing and controlling the world and of defying her mother's powers of endless transformation. She also has sex with Roland, the camera salesman, who reminds her of her father, wrapping up the day of taboo breaking by rushing from his bed to Paul's.

Then, as if in response, the mother invades Lucy's New York world. Lucy drapes a piece of fabric over her lamp, creating in her room a strange light, a "mingling of early dusk and the last remains of a faraway sunset" (120). The light and the feeling that comes over Lucy are reminiscent of scenes of obeah ceremonies found throughout Kincaid's work. Here Lucy realizes she is in "a state of no state" that is "a bad way to be—your spirit usually feels the void and will summon something to come in, usually something bad" (121). What is summoned up is Maude Quick, her mother's goddaughter, who arrives in the New York apartment, fragrant with clove, lime, and rose oil, the scents of an obeah bath. She had sometimes cared for Lucy as a child, and in her desire to control and infantilize Lucy, to tyrannize her with petty rules of health and conduct, Maude represents a crude imitation of the mother herself. We also know that in some sense Maude's visitation *is* the mother, come to break down Lucy's defiance by confronting her with the immensity of her guilt: Lucy has deserted her family in its time of tragedy; by ignoring her mother's letter she has ignored news of her father's death and her mother's grief and sudden poverty.

Lucy is nearly overcome, and we are reminded of the episode in *Annie John* in which the mother tries to get Annie to reveal the location of the hidden marbles by evoking her pity with a fearsome story of the mother's own childhood. Annie is so filled with love and pity that she is ready to turn over the marbles, but the mother, overconfident, reveals her strategy and destroys her nearly successful effect by asking for the marbles, "her voice warm and soft and treacherous" (*AJ*, 70). In *Lucy*, Maude does the same, giving a small, smug laugh as Lucy struggles with the news of her father's death and her mother's despair, remarking, "You really remind me of your mother" (123). At the brink of surrender, Lucy is pulled back; Maude's confidence that Lucy will respond as expected, that she is still the child of her mother, that she *is* her mother, reminds Lucy of the life-or-death struggle she is engaged in to forge an identity separate from the mother's. Maude's real mission is not to report the father's death but to recapture Lucy for the mother. Saved by Maude's self-assured observation, her little laugh, Lucy renews her grip on the lifeline of defiance, refusing the guilt and accusing the mother herself of betrayal. Later, in a letter to the mother, she proclaims that she will never come home. For good measure, she adds a brief description of how much she enjoys her new "life as a slut" (128). With this, Lucy appears to have won the battle, if not the war. The mother intrudes on Lucy's new life no more, leaving Lucy to mourn "the end of a love affair, perhaps the only true love in my whole life I would ever know" (132).

By the book's final chapter, Lucy has become aware that she is inventing herself, not like a scientist but like an artist, following her instincts, knowing herself by observing herself. She has eluded numerous attempts to reimprison her, certain that she must discover herself alone. Thus, she leaves Mariah and her surrogate mothering, loses interest in Paul just as he begins to think he "possesses" her, and begins to avoid Peggy, whose shallow model of defiance Lucy has outgrown. If Lucy is defined by anything now, it is her refusal to be defined. She does not follow Mariah's advice to view her dilemma in terms of "woman's role in society." She does not, as Dance suggests is the usual case with the protagonists of West Indian writers, see her life as split between her Caribbean home and the Western or European world (18–19). Rather, she sees herself to be in an entirely unknown new cosmos, one not explained by ready-made theories, a cosmos in which even the laws of physics break down. "My sense of time had changed," Lucy notes, "and I did not know if the day went by too quickly or too slowly" (154).

The triumph in *Annie John* is the girl's departure from Antigua, even if it is a triumph that is experienced as an "emptying out" (*AJ*, 148), and feels more like losing than winning. The triumph in *Lucy* is the achievement of solitude. Lucy has not only escaped those who would fashion her into a reflection of themselves, but she has also managed to avoid replacing those left behind with a new set of people who would use her in the same way, however subtle or unconscious their desire to do so might be. It is a triumph for Lucy to find herself alone at last, yet she is not happy. As with Annie's departure from her island home, Lucy's achievement of the solitude of her own apartment in a big, foreign city is accompanied by an immense sense of loss. Lucy has achieved what she always wanted; at the same time, she wants most passionately that which she has renounced, a love so great "that I would die from it." So great is the desire and the "shame" at being still so overwhelmed by it, so much does Lucy weep, that at the book's end her tears cause everything she has written in her beautiful new journal to dissolve into one big "blur" (164).

Yet, even if grief may at times blur the picture, Lucy is not, like the girl at the end of *Annie John*, entirely afloat in loss. Her new solitary life may be frightening, but it is still a life firmly grounded in domestic detail, the listing of which seems to be for Kincaid an invocation of home. Lucy cannot replicate her beautiful, powerful mother, but she can replicate the details of cooking, cleaning, and arranging that were the locus of life and love when mother and daughter were united. Here, then, in spite of the grief that blurs the words on the journal page, is Lucy, for the first time, mistress of her home, her own small world. After this world has been set to rights, furthermore, we hear an echo, albeit a strangely peaceful one, of the mother's voice that opens Kincaid's first story, "Girl": "I did all sorts of little things; I washed my underwear, scrubbed the stove, washed the bathroom floor, trimmed my nails, arranged my dresser, made sure I had enough sanitary napkins. When I got into bed, I lay there with the light on for a long time doing nothing" (163).

Chapter Nine

A Small Place: Masters and Slaves

In writing her long essay of postcolonial Antigua, *A Small Place*, published as a book in 1988, Kincaid made the most profound shift in her work to date. Gone are the surreal dreamscapes of *At the Bottom of the River*; gone is the gentle, sad tone of *Annie John*. Suddenly, in a move reminiscent of the abrupt, aggressive shift in the mother's voice in "Girl," the author, in the first part of the essay, wheels in accusation on readers, whom she assumes to be white and relatively privileged *New Yorker* subscribers, addressing them in an inescapable second person: "You are a tourist, a North American or European—to be frank, white" (4). An unrelenting attack takes up the first quarter of the 81-page essay. Kincaid shows the white tourist as repeating in the postcolonial age the pattern of racial and cultural domination begun by slaveholding European colonists. White tourists, Kincaid allows, may feel a few twinges of guilt when they visit a country like Antigua, a "slightly funny feeling" about "exploitation, oppression [and] domination" or the continued relationship of the so-called first world with the so-called third world. This feeling, if allowed to persist, could "ruin" a holiday (10), and to avoid such unpleasantness, the tourist is determined to see the black Antiguans as picturesque objects, rather than as thinking, feeling human beings. Kincaid is just as determined to reveal the Antiguans as subjects and to show exactly the sort of object the "incredibly unattractive, fat, pastrylike-fleshed" white tourist may appear to be in their eyes (13).

Having demonstrated for her readers how it feels to be turned into an object—and an inferior object, at that—Kincaid allows that the tourists may be "nice" and "attractive people" at home. It is only when they feel something missing in "the modern experience" (16) and seek to revive themselves by entering into the narcissistic role of tourist that they become ugly; only when seeking to reduce others to objects, to empty others of content, do they themselves become empty.

In the essay's short second section, Kincaid shows the connection between the contemporary white tourist and European imperialists who dominated the Caribbean for centuries. There were probably good

Europeans, Kincaid says, but they stayed home. Those who came to conquer new lands were, like the tourists, bent on escaping themselves by
dominating others. Fearing their own emptiness, they were—and are—
bolstered by their ability to empty others out, to turn others into objects,
literally in the case of slavery.

The white reader who can get through the first two sections—some
cannot, it seems, judging from the way in which reviews of the work frequently refer only to the first half—is in a sense rewarded in the second
half of the essay by an unusually and painfully frank portrait of the
postcolonial Caribbean and the way in which the new, native rulers continue the pattern of greed and oppression. Indeed, although a reviewer
for the London *Times Literary Supplement* amazingly stated that "what
Kincaid does not say" is that Antigua has had self-government for
decades (Fonseca), Kincaid devotes the bulk of the essay to precisely this,
a detailed account of the shambles that has been made of the island since
the end of colonial rule and the awful fear Kincaid feels that things may
be actually worse than before.

The essay was judged too "angry" for the *New Yorker* under Robert
Gottlieb (Perry interview 132), and a *New York Times* reviewer felt that
the essay is "distorted by anger" that "backs the reader into a corner"
(Hill). But Kincaid's method here may actually be the only way to communicate in such circumstances, for it is not only governmental corruption and incompetence she sees when she looks at her former home but
also an unsettling mixture of "innocence, art," and "lunacy" (68) in her
people. The mixture is puzzling, even to Kincaid, the result, over centuries, of both resistance to and the internalization of her people's
oppressors' view of them. Speaking of the Antiguans' relation to
tourism, Kincaid says that it is "as if, having observed the event of
tourism, they have absorbed it so completely that they have made the
degradation and humiliation of their daily lives into their own tourist
attraction" (69).

These are painful matters, Kincaid's method seems to indicate, not to
be discussed with people who must always see themselves in a favorable
light, who cannot be told that white people and white flesh can on occasion be viewed as unattractive. It is only with white readers who are willing to drop their sense of superiority—as is required to get through the
first half of the essay—and who are willing to consider their own continued participation in the domination of some groups by others that
Kincaid is willing to share her anguish over what she sees when she looks
back to her own home and people.

A Small Place does not back the white reader, to whom Kincaid speaks throughout, into a corner, but seeks to do the opposite, to allow him or her out of the corner of racial anxiety and paralysis by showing that what separates people is not, finally, racial difference. No one's essential nature is to be good or bad, Kincaid writes. Rather, all are dehumanized who allow themselves to be defined in terms of power relationships. And Kincaid works here to explain to white readers the incredibly complex effect, on white and black alike, of centuries of domination, showing them their own continued participation in a way that may not have been visible to them before. She is also trying to explain, to herself as well, what the psychological effects of slavery, colonialism, and their aftermath have been for the black residents of Antigua.

Here, as elsewhere in Kincaid's work, power is portrayed as narcissistic; the white tourists do not see the black islanders as people with lives and emotions of their own. Instead, the tourists reduce everyone and everything they see to a quaint, picturesque stereotype of third-world ineffectiveness that will enhance for the tourist the sense of really being on holiday: "Oh, what a marvellous change these bad roads are from the splendid highways I am used to in North America" (5). At the same time that the white tourist uses the islanders and their lives as decorative background for his vacation, he also uses them to assure himself of his own superiority. You the tourist, Kincaid says, are always secretly thinking that the Antiguans' "ancestors were not clever in the way yours were and not ruthless in the way yours were, for then would it not be you who would be in harmony with nature and backwards in that charming way?" (17).

Kincaid's aim in this section is to turn the tables, to demonstrate powerfully how it feels to be made into an object used by others for their amusement and the reinforcement of their own sense of superiority. Very soon the essay, which sounds in the beginning like a pleasurable piece of travel writing ("If you go to Antigua as a tourist, this is what you will see"), is thrown into reverse. Now the point is not what the tourist sees but how the tourist is seen by the natives; now it is not the tourist making condescending judgments of others but the tourist being judged. Kincaid's continuing address in the second person drives home the unpleasantness of this experience: "An ugly thing, that is what you are when you become a tourist, an ugly, empty thing, a stupid thing, a piece of rubbish pausing here and there to gaze at this and taste that, and it will never occur to you that the people who inhabit the place in which

you have just paused cannot stand you, that behind their closed doors
they laugh at your strangeness" (17).

For those who enter into a relationship in which they turn other people into objects, some spiritual quality of human connection is lost. Not
only do they turn others into objects, but they become objects themselves. All lose in this type of relationship, even when only the people on
the bottom are consciously aware of what is happening.

If white *New Yorker* readers can be made to understand the destructive
power relationship they enter when they become tourists in a place like
Antigua, then perhaps in the next section of *A Small Place* they can grasp
the vastly more destructive relationships of slavery and imperialism. To
Kincaid, the two spring from similar impulses. Like the tourist, who
wants to be renewed and refreshed among people too backward to have
entirely controlled nature, the European imperialist wanted to take raw
materials from the unspoiled "New World." In the extreme case of slavery, the people who were seen by their captors as less than human are
first robbed of all those things by which we know ourselves as human:
"What I see is the millions of people, of whom I am just one, made
orphans: no motherland, no fatherland, no gods, no mounds of earth for
holy ground, no excess of love which might lead to things that an excess
of love sometimes brings, and worst and most painful of all, no tongue.
(For isn't it odd that the only language I have in which to speak of this
crime is the language of the criminal who committed the crime?)" (31).

The effects of this theft live on, Kincaid believes, even though the
"criminal" is "shocked and surprised" when someone like her continues
to rail over something that happened many years ago. Indeed, Adewale
Maja-Pearce, writing in the British *New Statesman and Society*, advised
Kincaid to stop "snivelling" over the "sins" of the "long-departed colonial power" and to "reject the seductive condition of the victim" (40).
But the crime of slavery and colonialism, Kincaid maintains, the removal
of a group of people from all that told them who they were, is not over,
in spite of the colonialists' departure, "for this wrong can never be made
right . . . nothing can erase my rage" (32).

It is not only the British whom Kincaid takes to task here but also,
gently, as if in warm-up for the next section, the black Antiguans themselves. They do not seem to grasp fully what has happened, and continues to happen, to them, Kincaid believes. They still do not see the
English as racists but simply as people with deplorable manners, and
they do not understand that their own good behavior is the "posture of
the weak, of children" (30). She remembers, for instance, standing in

"hot sun for hours so that I could see a putty-faced Princess from England disappear" behind the high white wall that surrounded Government House. She is shocked, as she looks back, at how "cowed we must have been," so that no one "ever wrote bad things" on the wall; "it remained clean and white and high" (25). Critics like Maja-Pearce notwithstanding, Kincaid is determined that the picture of colonialism be defaced, even if belatedly.

In the essay's third and longest section, Kincaid attempts to draw a picture of the personality fostered by centuries of domination. To do this, she explores the paradox that seems to entrap Antiguans. She sees that she and other Antiguans have been seduced by a story taught them by the colonial powers, learning to love this story before becoming aware that it is erasing them as human beings. When the story is shown to be false, subjects of colonialism are left with an immense sense of loss, so overwhelming that they try to cling to the old beliefs, though on some level they now know how destructive it is to do so.

This paradox, as Kincaid understands, seems to entrap even the writer herself as she considers the destruction of the island's library in an earthquake in 1974. Still standing but unrepaired and unusable, it serves as a metaphor for colonial power and its aftermath. Kincaid clearly loved the old library, and her heart breaks at the makeshift affair, the "dung heap" (43), that has replaced it. At the same time, she is fully aware that the library's primary function was to acquaint the Antiguan reader with the British in all their "greatness" and "beauty" and to justify all of their actions. In lamenting the library, Kincaid laments not only the "corruption" of postcolonial government and a general sense of "things gone bad" but also the loss of a dream that was as beautiful as it was treacherously seductive:

But if you saw the old library, situated as it was, in a big, old wooden building painted a shade of yellow that is beautiful to people like me, with its wide veranda, its big, always open windows, its rows and rows of shelves filled with books, its beautiful wooden tables and chairs for sitting and reading, if you could hear the sound of its quietness (for the quiet in this library was a sound in itself), the smell of the sea (which was a stone's throw away), the heat of the sun (no building could protect us from that), the beauty of us sitting there like communicants at an altar, taking in, again and again, the fairy tale of how we met you, your right to do the things you did, how beautiful you were, are, and always will be; if you could see all of that in just one glimpse, you would see why my heart would break at the dung heap that now passes for a library in Antigua. (42–43)

As Kincaid cannot stop loving the library and the stories of the beautiful British it contained, the Antiguans she meets on a visit there seem
unable to let go of the other great story to which they are heir, that of
slavery. On her return trip, she notices that people are "obsessed" with
slavery, speaking of it

> as if it had been a pageant full of large ships sailing on blue water, the
> large ships filled up with human cargo—their ancestors; they got off,
> they were forced to work under conditions that were cruel and inhuman,
> they were beaten, they were murdered, they were sold, their children
> were taken from them and these separations lasted forever, there were
> many other bad things, and then suddenly the whole thing came to an
> end in something called emancipation. Then they speak of emancipation
> itself as if it happened just the other day, not over one hundred and fifty
> years ago. The word "emancipation" is used so frequently, it is as if,
> emancipation, were a contemporary occurrence, something everybody is
> familiar with. (54–55)

People in Antigua, Kincaid writes, do not see a connection between
their "obsession with slavery"; their pride in the Hotel Training School,
which seems to be the island's chief educational institution; and "the fact
that they are governed by corrupt men, or that these corrupt men have
given their country away to corrupt foreigners" (55). Kincaid has not
spelled out this connection, yet it seems to be part of the same paradox
mentioned above. People can be made to love and then find themselves
clinging to a self-destructive fantasy. The story of slavery—the big ships,
the blue seas, the simple tale of victimization, the simple triumph of
emancipation—controls identity for many Antiguans. But they do not
examine this story and the relation it may have to their present lives.
Rather, they seem content to look, mesmerized by its grand drama. As a
result, they do not learn anything from the story of slavery and thus do
not get past it. Degradation continues to be their deepest identity, and
so they celebrate the institution that teaches their sons and daughters to
be servants to rich tourists. Graduation ceremonies, Kincaid reports, are
televised.

Ultimately, what seems to strike Kincaid most when she visits her
country after decades of absence is that while an enormous amount of
energy is devoted to trivial, everyday occurrences, very little energy is
devoted to examining the forces, past and present, that determine how
Antiguans will live their lives. Rather, any question of real importance is

"assembled (artfully) into a picture story" (57). Kincaid asks, "Might not knowing why they are the way they are, why they do the things they do, why they live the way they live and in the place they live, why the things that happened to them happened, lead these people to a different relationship with the world, a more demanding relationship, a relationship in which they are not victims all the time of every bad idea that flits across the mind of the world?" (56–57).

Finally, Kincaid is herself bewildered by the attitude she finds among her own people, the strangely disengaged voice with which they tell the litany of disasters that continue to befall them and their small country. Do they, she wonders, live on a higher plane than those who "understand" how things happen in the world, how events are connected? Or have they been driven insane by their hideously unexamined experience? "I look at these people [Antiguans], and I cannot tell whether I was brought up by, and so come from, children, eternal innocents, or artists who have not yet found eminence in a world too stupid to understand, or lunatics who have made their own lunatic asylum, or an exquisite combination of all three" (57).

Kincaid's own people seem to be more of a continuing mystery to her than are her white readers. Nevertheless, her prescription for both is the same. Only by seeing the role one has taken in an environment ordered by power relationships and by being determined to throw off that role can one become fully human: "Of course, the whole thing is, once you cease to be a master, once you throw off your master's yoke, you are no longer human rubbish, you are just a human being, and all the things that adds up to. So, too, with the slaves. Once they are no longer slaves, once they are free they are no longer noble and exalted; they are just human beings" (81).

Notes and References

Chapter One

1. Jamaica Kincaid, *At the Bottom of the River* (New York: Plume, 1992), 12 (originally published in the *New Yorker*); hereafter cited in the text as *BR*.

2. Jamaica Kincaid, *Annie John* (New York: Plume, 1986), 76 (originally published in the *New Yorker*); hereafter cited in the text as *AJ*.

3. Craig Tapping, "Children and History in the Caribbean Novel: George Lamming's *In the Castle of My Skin* and Jamaica Kincaid's *Annie John*," *Kunapipi* 11, no. 2 (1989): 53.

4. Jamaica Kincaid, *A Small Place* (New York: Farrar, Straus and Giroux, 1988), 17; hereafter cited in the text as *SP*.

5. Jamaica Kincaid, *Lucy* (New York: Farrar, Straus and Giroux, 1990), 91 (originally published in the *New Yorker*); hereafter cited in the text.

6. Anne Tyler, "Mothers and Mysteries," *New Republic* (31 December 1983): 33; hereafter cited in the text.

7. Giovanna Covi, "Jamaica Kincaid and the Resistance to Canons," in *Out of the Kumbla: Caribbean Women and Literature*, ed. Carole Boyce Davies and Elaine Savory Fido (Trenton, N.J.: Africa World Press, 1990), 348–49; hereafter cited in the text.

8. Jacqueline Austin, "Up from Eden," *Village Voice Literary Supplement* (April 1985): 7; hereafter cited in the text.

9. Leslie Garis, "Through West Indian Eyes," *New York Times Magazine*, 7 October 1990, 80; hereafter cited in the text.

10. Louis James, "Reflections and the Bottom of the River: The Transformation of Caribbean Experience in the Fiction of Jamaica Kincaid," *Wasafiri* (Winter 1988–89): 15.

11. Jamaica Kincaid, interview with author, Bennington, Vt., 12 June 1993; hereafter cited in the text as Simmons.

12. Jamaica Kincaid, "Jamaica Kincaid's New York," *Rolling Stone*, 6 October 1977, 73; hereafter cited in the text as "JKNY."

13. Selwyn Cudjoe, "Jamaica Kincaid and the Modernist Project: An Interview," *Callaloo* 12, no. 2 (Spring 1989): 399; hereafter cited in the text.

14. Jamaica Kincaid, "Notes and Comment," from "The Talk of the Town," *New Yorker*, 17 October 1977, 37.

15. Jamaica Kincaid, "Notes and Comment," from "The Talk of the Town," *New Yorker*, 3 January 1983, 24.

16. Jamaica Kincaid, "Notes and Comment," from "The Talk of the Town," *New Yorker*, 19 July 1976, 23.

17. Jamaica Kincaid, "Antigua Crossing," *Rolling Stone*, 29 June 1978, 48; hereafter cited in the text.

18. Jamaica Kincaid, "On Seeing England for the First Time," *Harper's* (August 1991): 14 (originally published in the journal *Transition* and later reprinted in the 1992 edition of *Best American Essays*, ed. Susan Sontag); hereafter cited in the text as "SE."

19. Allan Vorda, "An Interview With Jamaica Kincaid," *Mississippi Review* 20 (1991): 15; hereafter cited in the text.

20. Jamaica Kincaid, "Flowers of Evil," from "In the Garden," *New Yorker*, 5 October 1992, 159; hereafter cited in the text as "Flowers."

21. Charlotte Brontë, *Jane Eyre* (1847; repr., New York: Viking Penguin, 1985), 215; hereafter cited in the text.

22. Jamaica Kincaid, "Last of the Black White Girls," *Village Voice*, 28 June 1976, 150; hereafter cited in the text as "Last."

23. Donna Perry, "Jamaica Kincaid," *Backtalk: Women Writers Speak Out: Interviews with Donna Perry* (New Brunswick, N.J.: Rutgers University Press, 1993), 133; hereafter cited in the text as Perry interview.

24. Jamaica Kincaid and George Trow, "West Indian Weekend" from "The Talk of the Town," *New Yorker*, 30 September 1974, 30–31.

25. Hilary DeVries, *Christian Science Monitor*, 2 May 1985, 41.

26. Audrey Edwards, "Jamaica Kincaid Writes of Passage," *Essence* (May 1991): 87; hereafter cited in the text.

27. Susan Sontag, jacket copy for *At the Bottom of the River*.

28. Derek Walcott, jacket copy for *At the Bottom of the River*.

29. Paula Bonnell, "Annie Travels to Second Childhood," *Boston Herald*, 31 March 1985, 126.

30. Salman Rushdie, quoted in Richard Locke, "An Antiguan Girl in America," *Wall Street Journal*, 16 October 1990, A24.

31. Michiko Kakutani, "Portrait of Antigua, Warts and All," *New York Times*, 16 July 1988, 15.

32. Alison Friesinger Hill, *New York Times Book Review*, 10 July 1988, 19; hereafter cited in the text.

33. Adewale Maja-Pearce, "Corruption in the Caribbean," *New Statesman and Society*, 7 October 1988, 40; hereafter cited in the text.

34. Thulani Davis, "Girl-Child in a Foreign Land," *New York Times Book Review*, 28 October 1990, 11.

35. Jane Mendelsohn, "Leaving Home: Jamaica Kincaid's Voyage Round Her Mother," *Village Voice Literary Supplement* (October 1990): 21.

36. Jamaica Kincaid, "Song of Roland," *New Yorker*, 12 April 1993, 95.

Chapter Two

1. Alice Miller, *The Drama of the Gifted Child: How Narcissistic Parents Form and Deform the Emotional Lives of Their Talented Children*, trans. Ruth Ward (New York: Basic Books, 1981), 35 (originally published as *Prisoners of Childhood*); hereafter cited in the text.

2. Nancy Chodorow, "Family Structure and Feminine Personality," in *Women, Culture, and Society*, ed. Michelle Z. Rosaldo and Louise Lamphere (Stanford, Calif.: Stanford University Press, 1974), 48; hereafter cited in the text.

3. Patricia Hill Collins, "The Meaning of Motherhood in Black Culture and Black Mother-Daughter Relationships," *Sage* 4, no. 2 (Fall 1987): 3–10; hereafter cited in the text.

4. While Chodorow's article concerns itself primarily with describing the mother-daughter relationship found in Western, middle-class societies, characterized by mothers who see their daughters as "narcissistic extensions or doubles of themselves" (48), she also notes the existence of "matrifocal" societies, giving examples from Java, Moslem Morocco, and working-class East London. In these societies, where strong relationships between women are expressed through "mutual cooperation and frequent contact, . . . the people surrounding a mother while a child is growing up become mediators between mother and daughter, by providing a daughter with alternative models for personal identification and objects of attachment, which contribute to her differentiation from her mother" (63).

5. Brenda O. Daly and Maureen T. Reddy, eds., *Narrating Mothers: Theorizing Maternal Subjectivities* (Knoxville: University of Tennessee Press, 1991), 8.

6. Helen Pyne Timothy, "Adolescent Rebellion and Gender Relations in *At the Bottom of the River* and *Annie John*," in *Caribbean Women Writers: Essays from the First International Conference*, ed. Selwyn Cudjoe (Wellesley, Mass.: Calaloux Publications, 1990), 240; hereafter cited in the text.

Chapter Three

1. Edith Milton, "Making a Virtue of Diversity," *New York Times Book Review*, 15 January 1984, 22; hereafter cited in the text.

2. Houston A. Baker, Jr., *Modernism and the Harlem Renaissance* (Chicago: University of Chicago Press, 1987), 43; hereafter cited in the text.

3. Charles W. Chesnutt, *The Conjure Woman* (1899; repr., Ann Arbor: University of Michigan Press, 1969); hereafter cited in the text.

4. Isabel Fonseca, "Their Island Story," *Times Literary Supplement* (London), 13 January 1989, 30; hereafter cited in the text.

5. Susan Kenney, "Paradise With Snake," *New York Times Book Review*, 7 April 1985, 6; hereafter cited in the text.

6. Donna Perry, "Initiation in Jamaica Kincaid's *Annie John*," in Cudjoe, *Caribbean Women Writers*, 250; hereafter cited in the text.

7. Suzanne Freeman, "Three Short-Story Collections with a Difference," *MS* 12 (January 1984): 16.

8. David Leavitt, "Brief Encounters," *Village Voice*, 17 January 1984, 41.

9. Jamaica Kincaid, "Ovando," *Conjunctions* 14 (1989): 75–83; hereafter cited in the text.

10. Hilton Als, "Don't Worry, Be Happy," *Nation*, 18 February 1991, 209.

11. Peggy Ellsberg, "Rage Laced with Lyricism," *Commonweal*, 4 November 1988, 604.

12. Toni Morrison, "The Site of Memory," *Inventing the Truth: The Art and Craft of Memoir*, ed. William Zinsser (Boston: Houghton Mifflin, 1987), 113.

13. Marjorie Pryse, "Zora Neale Hurston, Alice Walker, and the 'Ancient Power' of Black Women," in *Conjuring: Black Women, Fiction, and Literary Tradition*, ed. Marjorie Pryse and Hortense J. Speillers (Bloomington: Indiana University Press, 1983), 6.

Chapter Five

1. Françoise Lionnet, *Autobiographical Voices: Race, Gender, Self-Portraiture* (Ithaca, N.Y.: Cornell University Press, 1989), 3; hereafter cited in the text.

2. John Milton, *Paradise Lost*, in *The Norton Anthology of English Literature*, 5th ed., vol. 1, ed. M. H. Abrams (New York: W. W. Norton, 1986), 1449; hereafter cited in the text.

3. Sandra M. Gilbert and Susan Gubar, *The Mad Woman in the Attic* (New Haven, Conn.: Yale University Press, 1979), 339.

4. Penny Broumelha, *Charlotte Brontë* (Bloomington: Indiana University Press, 1990), 61.

Chapter Six

1. "Notes and Comment," from "The Talk of the Town," *New Yorker*, 3 January 1983, 23.

Chapter Seven

1. Paula Bonnell,"'Annie' Travels to Second Childhood," *Boston Herald*, 31 March 1985, 126.

2. Ike Onwordi, "Wising Up," *Times Literary Supplement* (London), 29 November 1985, 1374.

3. Helen Tiffin, "Decolonization and Audience: Erna Brodber's *Myal*

and Jamaica Kincaid's *A Small Place,*" *Span* 30 (1990): 31; hereafter cited in the text.

4.   J. D. Salinger, *The Catcher in the Rye* (1951; repr., New York: Bantam, 1989), 1; hereafter cited in the text.

5.   Daryl Cumber Dance, "Go Eena Kumbla: A Comparison of Erna Brodber's *Jane and Louisa Will Soon Come Home* and Toni Cade Bambera's *The Salt Eaters,*" in Cudjoe, *Caribbean Women Writers,* 170–71.

6.   Erna Brodber, *Jane and Louisa Will Soon Come Home* (London: New Beacon Books, 1980), 23–24.

7.   Merle Hodge, *Crick Crack, Monkey* (1970; repr., London: Heinemann Educational Books, 1981), 61.

8.   Here and elsewhere in Kincaid's writing, parallels to Lewis Carroll's *Alice* are striking, even though Kincaid does not acknowledge, and I do not mean to imply, any particular debt to Carroll. Asked by interviewer Allan Vorda whether her writing owes a debt to "other writers of magical realism, such as Borges or Marquez and even possibly Lewis Carroll," Kincaid replied, "If it went back to anyone it would be Lewis Carroll." She added, *"The truth is I come from a place that's very unreal.* . . . The place I come from goes off in fantasy all the time, so that every event is continually a spectacle. . . . I wouldn't say that I was influenced by these other writers you mentioned, because for me, it's only an accident. It's really the place I grew up in. I'm not really a very imaginative writer, but the reality of my background is fantastic" (13).

Chapter Eight

1.   Daryl Cumber Dance, *Fifty Caribbean Writers: A Bio-bibliographical and Critical Sourcebook* (Westport, Conn.: Greenwood Press, 1986); hereafter cited in the text.

2.   Lewis Carroll, *Alice's Adventures in Wonderland* (1865; repr., London: J. M. Dent, 1954), 5.

Selected Bibliography

PRIMARY WORKS

Collected Fiction

At the Bottom of the River. New York: Farrar, Straus and Giroux, 1983.
Annie John. New York: Farrar, Straus and Giroux, 1985.
Lucy. New York: Farrar, Straus and Giroux, 1990.
Autobiography of My Mother. Farrar, Straus and Giroux, scheduled for publication in Fall, 1994.

Uncollected Fiction

"Antigua Crossing." *Rolling Stone*, 29 June 1978, 48–50.
"Ovando." *Conjunctions* 14 (1989): 75–83.
"Song of Roland." *New Yorker*, 12 April 1993, 94–98.

Nonfiction

"Jamaica Kincaid's New York." *Rolling Stone*, 6 October 1977, 71–73.
A Small Place. New York: Farrar, Straus and Giroux, 1988.
"On Seeing England for the First Time." *Harper's* (August 1991), 13–17.
"Flowers of Evil." From "In the Garden," *New Yorker*, 5 October 1992, 154–59.
"A Fire by Ice." From "In the Garden," *New Yorker*, 22 February 1993, 64–67.
"Just Reading." From "In the Garden," *New Yorker*, 29 March 1993, 51–54.
"Alien Soil." From "In the Garden," *New Yorker*, 21 June 1993, 47–51.
"This Other Eden." From "In the Garden," *New Yorker*, 23 and 30 August 1993, 69–73.

SECONDARY WORKS

Chapters in Books

Covi, Giovanna. "Jamaica Kincaid and the Resistance to Canons." In *Out of the Kumbla: Caribbean Women and Literature*, edited by Carole Boyce Davies and Elaine Savory Fido, 345–54. Trenton, N.J.: Africa World Press, 1990. A postmodernist reading of Kincaid, particularly influenced by Jacques Derrida and Julia Kristeva.
Mangum, Bryant. "Jamaica Kincaid." In *Fifty Caribbean Writers: A Bio-bibliographical Critical Source Book*, edited by Daryl Cumber Dance, 255–63.

New York: Greenwood Press, 1986. A brief examination of the themes found in Kincaid's first two books of fiction.

Perry, Donna, ed. "Jamaica Kincaid." In *Backtalk: Women Writers Speak Out: Interviews by Donna Perry*, 127–41. New Brunswick, N.J.: Rutgers University Press, 1983. Kincaid discusses political themes in her work.

———. "Initiation in Jamaica Kincaid's *Annie John*." In *Caribbean Women Writers: Essays from the First International Conference*, edited by Selwyn Cudjoe, 245–53. Wellesley, Mass.: Calaloux Publications, 1990. The discussion centers on the myths and traditions of women of color and third-world women.

Timothy, Helen Pyne. "Adolescent Rebellion and Gender Relations in *At the Bottom of the River* and *Annie John*." In *Caribbean Women Writers: Essays from the First International Conference*, edited by Selwyn Cudjoe, 233–42. Wellesley, Mass.: Calaloux Publications, 1990. An examination of the mother-daughter rift in Kincaid's work.

Journal Articles

Cudjoe, Selwyn R. "Jamaica Kincaid and the Modernist Project: An Interview." *Callaloo* 12 (Spring 1989): 396–411. A long interview containing a great deal of biographical information.

Dutton, Wendy. "Merge and Separate: Jamaica Kincaid's Fiction." *World Literature Today* 63 (Summer 1989): 406–10. Kincaid's first two books of fiction read as studies in female growth and power.

Garis, Leslie. "Through West Indian Eyes." *New York Times Magazine*, 7 October 1990, 42. A medium-length interview in which Kincaid discusses the controversy surrounding publication of *Lucy*.

James, Louis. "Reflections, and the Bottom of the River: The Transformation of Caribbean Experience in the Fiction of Jamaica Kincaid." *Wasafiri* 89 (Winter 1988): 15–17. Examines questions of illusion and reality in Kincaid's early fiction.

Murdoch, H. Adlai. "Severing the (M)other Connection: The Representation of Cultural Identity in Jamaica Kincaid's *Annie John*." *Callaloo* 13 (1990): 325–40. A Lacanian reading of the quest for identity in *Annie John*.

Natov, Roni. "Mothers and Daughters: Jamaica Kincaid's Pre-Oedipal Narrative." *Children's Literature* 18 (1990): 1–16. Examines the mother-daughter connection in Kincaid's first two works of fiction.

Simmons, Diane. "The Mother Mirror in Jamaica Kincaid's *Annie John* and Gertrude Stein's *The Good Anna*." In *The Anna Book: Searching for Anna in Literary History*, edited by Mickey Pearlman (Westport, Conn.: Greenwood Press, 1992), 99–104.

Tapping, Craig. "Children and History in the Caribbean Novel: George Lamming's *In the Castle of My Skin* and Jamaica Kincaid's *Annie John*."

Kunapipi 9 (1989): 51–59. A postcolonial reading sees Kincaid's *Annie John* as questioning the authoritative version of Caribbean history.

Tiffin, Helen. "Decolonization and Audience: Erna Brodber's *Myal* and Jamaica Kincaid's *A Small Place*." *Span* 30 (1990): 27–38. Examines the relationship of story and audience in the colonial and postcolonial context of Kincaid's essay.

Vorda, Allan. "An Interview with Jamaica Kincaid." *Mississippi Review* 20 (1991): 7–26. The writer discusses themes and characters in *Lucy*.

Index

The Author

Diane Simmons's second novel, *Dreams Like Thunder*, won the 1993 Oregon Book Award for fiction. She holds a Ph.D. in English from the City University of New York where her doctoral dissertation on Jamaica Kincaid won the Melvin Dixon prize for best dissertation on African-American literature. She is an assistant professor of English at Upsala College in East Orange, New Jersey.

The Editor

Frank Day is a professor of English and department head at Clemson University. He is the author of *Sir William Empson: An Annotated Bibliography* and *Arthur Koestler: A Guide to Research*. He was a Fulbright Lecturer in American literature in Romania (1980–81) and in Bangladesh (1986–87).